CONTENTS

Introduction		5
Chapter 1	Life's Bottom Line	11
Chapter 2	Batting 1.000 in the Game of Life	35
Chapter 3	Keeping the Faith	59
Chapter 4	Impressions, Impressions	83
Chapter 5	A Lesson From the Gulf War	107
Chapter 6	Are You For Real?	131
Conclusion		158

*How to have an authentic faith
in a faithless society*

KNOWING
GOD
IN THE
REAL WORLD

JON PAULIEN

Pacific Press® Publishing Association
Nampa, Idaho
Oshawa, Ontario, Canada

Edited by B. Russell Holt
Designed by Dennis Ferree
Cover photo by Stephen Johnson/STONE Photo

Copyright © 2000 by
Pacific Press® Publishing Association
Printed in the United States of America

Unless otherwise noted, New Testament Scripture quotations are
personal translations by the author, Old Testament Scripture quotations are taken from the New International Version.

Library of Congress Cataloging-in-Publication Data

Paulien, Jon, 1949-
    Knowing God in the real world: how to have an authentic faith in a faith-
less society./Jon Paulien.
        p. cm.
    ISBN 0-8163-1812-3
    1. Christian life—Seventh-day Adventist authors. I. Title.

BV4501.2.P38 2001
248.4'86732—dc21   00-046479

00 01 02 03 04 • 5 4 3 2 1

INTRODUCTION

In 1993 Pacific Press published my book *Present Truth in the Real World*. That book called the Seventh-day Adventist Church to take a fresh look at its mission. Seventh-day Adventists believe that they have a mission to the entire world, to prepare the world for the second coming of Jesus. We have tried to grow the Church in all parts of the world to accomplish that mission. And we have been very good at it.

Present Truth, however, pointed out some painful realities. While the membership of the Church has been growing, its *penetration* into all levels of society has actually been shrinking. We have had little impact on the vast worlds of Islam, Buddhism, and Hinduism. We have had little impact on the secularized masses of Europe and Australia. Even in the relatively Christian United States, our message is noticed primarily by those in the working classes who already have an interest in the Bible—particularly the book of Revelation. Our evangelism has made little or no impact on the secular mainstream of American society.

So the predecessor of this book, *Present Truth in the Real World*, focused particularly on the issue of method. It examined how we might change a situation in which our Church is growing in most places, yet is having very little impact on the majority culture. How do we approach secular people, in particular, in such a way that they will take us seriously? What kinds of churches and what kinds of witnessing approaches are most effective with secular people? (I define "secular people" as individuals who in practice, not necessarily in belief, go about their everyday lives without reference to God. They are not atheists or agnostics; they simply don't find the concepts of God and church worth the time and effort many people put into them.) How do we manage to keep our own faith strong while living in the midst of a world that either ignores or disrespects our faith?

The response to my earlier book has been very gratifying. I wrote primarily for the North American scene, yet the book has been warmly received on nearly every continent. It has had a powerful effect on the way Seventh-day Adventist administrators, pastors, and lay people all over the world are looking at the mission of the Church. In spite of the painful analysis of where we are, Adventists everywhere, I have found, are hungry for an honest and truthful look at reality.

When I wrote *Present Truth*, I was aware that many thinkers believed that secularism was on its way out as a guiding philosophy of existence. That such spiritual movements as New Age and Islamic Fundamentalism signaled a general return to religious significance in society as a whole. Secularism was thought to be self-limiting in practice. As people discovered that life without God has no meaning, they would return to faith and spirituality. Therefore, at the time I wrote, I expected that my book on the impact of secularism might have a very limited shelf life.

The expectation that secularism would be reversed has proven to be at least partly right. Spirituality and faith are much more a part of everyday consciousness than they were ten years ago, especially in the media. People are more comfortable talking casually about their spiritual commitments. I find this to be true in Adventist congregations and educational centers as well. People, both inside and outside of the church, are hungry to touch the substance behind the doctrines, institutions, and forms in which faith has been expressed. This hunger was not nearly so obvious ten years ago.

At the same time, however, Christian churches have not found their challenges diminishing. Although faith and spirituality are held in higher esteem, religion in general is not. Faith and spirituality, as commonly understood, have made a certain peace with secular thinking so that faith and secularism can exist side-by-side without bothering anyone. But strong convictions remain suspect. Criticism of other faiths is considered out of line. Most of the insights in the previous book, therefore, are still right on the mark even though the specific context of society has changed somewhat.

Since the publication of *Present Truth,* many people have expressed the wish that I had not limited myself primarily to *method* and had said more about the matter of *message*. They have felt that a major barrier, or even *the* major barrier, to reaching secular people is the fact that the message we bring has been expressed in language that does not make sense to people in the mainstream of today's society. I promised to continue giving the matter of message more thought and that I would eventually write a book on the kind of message that would make sense to secular people without compromising the clear teachings of Scripture. This book is an initial attempt in that direction.

In this book I address Christianity 101—what is the bottom line in Christian faith? But it's more than just the bottom line. How can the basics of the gospel be expressed in a way that makes sense in the secular world? This book examines the issue of salvation at a personal level. How do people get right with God? Is the Bible reasonably clear on the subject? Why should anyone want to have a relationship with God? What does it mean to have a relationship with someone you cannot see, hear, or touch? How can I truly know God in the real world? What does it mean to pray in a computerized world? Does God still communicate directly with people today? How can I have an authentic walk with God that will make a difference in today's world? What difference does it make to know Him?

These are some of the questions we will address in this book, *Knowing God in the Real World*. While each of the six chapters can, to some degree, stand on its own, there is an intentional progression through the book. The first chapter, "Life's Bottom Line," articulates the gospel in terms of the world we know today. Its purpose is to show that the gospel not only makes a difference, it is the only lasting solution to the fundamental issue of human existence. The second chapter, "Batting 1.000 in the Game of Life," clarifies the biblical balance of the gospel by unpacking a clear and specific text, Romans 3:23-25, in its context. The gospel cannot be fully appreciated when confused or unbalanced expressions of the gospel sidetrack seekers.

The third chapter, "Keeping the Faith," addresses the broad question of how to maintain a living relationship with One we cannot see, hear, or touch. Christian life is about more than a one-time acceptance of the Cross. Christian life is a living and ongoing experience with the same Jesus who died on that cross 2,000 years ago. Because prayer so often proves to be a struggle for people who are influenced by secular thinking, the fourth and fifth chapters offer practical suggestions for making prayer a more dynamic part of everyday experience.

The final chapter, "Are You For Real?", explores how a growing relationship with God affects even the deepest thoughts, feelings, and motivations. It applies the gospel to the hidden recesses of our experience. No experience with God will ever have a significant impact on secular society unless it is authentic and makes a difference in every aspect of our lives.

Before I close this *Introduction*, I'd like to say something about the intended audience for this book. *Knowing God in the Real World* is not addressed directly to secular people. I seriously doubt that such a book would be useful to secular readers, were I to write one. Secular people pay little attention to the various evangelistic "gimmicks" that we so carefully prepare for them. They are best reached, not by books or televised evangelism, but by one-on-one relationships with genuine, Spirit-filled Christians. This book, therefore, does not offer an evangelistic short-cut that addresses secular people directly. Its goal is to affect the understanding and the experience of those who know and care about secular people. Only when we know and experience the gospel for ourselves, can we hope to have any significant impact in the lives of secular persons. This book is not addressed, therefore, directly to secular people, but to two other audiences instead.

1. To those who may have contact with Christian faith, but who are looking for a deeper relationship with God. This audience may include active church members who may not be clear on the basics of salvation or on what it means to have a living relationship with God. To such believers the concept of a living walk with God may seem like an empty cliché, something that sounds pious but doesn't really work in practice. For them, a fresh, contemporary approach to basic Christianity may provide the necessary key to a genuine and fulfilling relationship with God.

Introduction

2. To those Christians who want to be better equipped to share the "good news of salvation" in the real world. Many Seventh-day Adventists and many other Christians know God personally but have difficulty sharing that knowledge in a meaningful way in the mainstream of our technological society. *Knowing God in the Real World* is a book for those who may know how to "drive a car," but who don't know how to communicate that knowledge to the kind of people they associate with every day.

I would encourage those who find a more meaningful experience of the gospel in these pages to review my earlier book, *Present Truth in the Real World*, for tools to help them apply that experience with those for whom the gospel makes little sense. The *message* focus of this book is the natural sequel to *Present Truth*'s focus on *method*. It is my prayer that God will use both these books to energize a movement that will reach the unreached as never before.

CHAPTER

1

LIFE'S BOTTOM LINE

When secular people see a bumper sticker or a billboard that says, "Jesus Is the Answer," they are rarely moved to reconsider the direction of their lives. They don't feel an urge to pull over to the side of the road, kneel down, and thank God for His answer to the problems in their lives. They will either ignore the message and its implications or respond with a flippant, "What do you suppose the question is?" Even if they are aware of serious issues in their lives, even if they have some sense of what the question is, secular people generally do not expect to find the answer in church or in Jesus.

Is there some way to bring the gospel home to a secular person so that it makes sense? Is the gospel as relevant today as it ever was? What difference does it make? In this chapter I would like to share with you a contemporary presentation of the gospel that has made some sense to the secular people I encounter from time to time.

Sticks and stones

Remember that childhood verse: "Sticks and stones may break my bones, but words will never hurt me"? Doesn't that sound like the stupidest proverb you've ever heard? It really isn't true, is it? Grown men, who would put up with all kinds of physical pain for a good cause, will often fall apart if you put them into a room full of people who are laughing at them.

Story of Pain & rejection

When I was young, I was a pretty tough guy. When I was fourteen years old, I had already developed a big, bass voice, and I had reached my full height and weight (well, I guess I *have* added a little weight in the last few years). That gave me a huge advantage on the football field during high school days. I remember those athletic days with some satisfaction now that I have reached middle age and things are not quite the way they were. But there was one day that has left a very different kind of memory.

It was my senior year of academy, and we had an awesome flagball team. I was the captain and the quarterback. My halfback was Danny, incredibly quick and shifty. He was a master at offering tacklers a look at his flag and then moving it away just when the other person reached for it. My fullback was Oscar—he was something else. He was even bigger and tougher than I was; I can remember him knocking two or three people out of my way and still looking around for somebody else to block. At the tight end position was Carlos. He was as big as Oscar, and he had great hands. All I had to do was to throw the ball into a crowd, and Carlos would somehow come out with it. Then there was Jaime, my wide receiver. He was 6'3" and 130 pounds, the fastest guy I ever saw outside of the pros.

We were great! I was throwing fairly well, and we were rolling up some big scores. Everything was going well except for one rule at that school: the captains of teams that were not playing had to referee the other games. That's OK up to a point, but things started going sour when the Bible teacher broke his ankle. He had been the quarterback of our biggest rivals, and now he was a spectator whenever his favorite team played. This man was my hero. He was the most admired man in my life. He was teaching me to know the Lord. He was the model of everything that I wanted to become someday—a teacher, a friend, and a man of God. Until that day.

That day I had to referee a game that his team was playing, and he stood with his crutches on the sideline. It wasn't long before I could hear his voice. "That was a dumb call! What's the matter, are you blind or something?" Time and again he had something to say about the quality of my refereeing. I tried my best to ignore him, but the impact of the comments began to pile up as the game went on.

"Oh, come on, that was obvious! Are you asleep on your feet?" "I've never seen such a ridiculous display of refereeing in my whole life!"

I thought I was handling it OK until a particular play in the third quarter. A power sweep ended up right on the sideline, right in front of him. I was in on top of the play and did my best to make the right call. He hollered angrily, "I don't believe it! I'm standing right here. I'm looking right at it. Are you stupid? Are you blind? What is your problem?"

I turned to him, and with trembling in my voice I said, "Look, I'm doing the best I can."

He looked me right in the eye for a couple of seconds, and then said with disgust in his voice, "*Your* best isn't good enough."

That game was played in a little field in the middle of a major city. I picked up the football and in fury threw the greatest spiral of my life. It landed on the top of a nearby building. I walked off the field with my head down. I found the deepest and darkest corner of the basement in that school, and I cried for two solid hours. Danny, Oscar, Carlos, and Jaime all followed me down to the basement to offer their support, but it didn't help. I cried, and I cried, and no one could stop me. My friends tried to tell me that the Bible teacher didn't really mean it and that he would apologize the next day (he never did), but it didn't help. Why?

What are you worth?

Why would a tough guy like me cry in front of his friends for two hours? How is it that words, mere words, can be so painful? It has to do with self-esteem or self-worth—how we feel about ourselves deep down inside. It seems that if the most admired person in your life thinks that *your best isn't good enough*, a little voice deep inside of you says, "Your best will *never* be good enough. Your life is over. You're a failure. You'll never amount to anything."

Self-worth, whether or not we realize it, is very important to the kind of life we live. How we feel about ourselves largely determines how we treat other people and how we face the major issues of life. Unless we can find a way to develop a strong, positive sense of what we are worth, everything we do will be negatively affected. Therefore, the search for a solid sense of what we are worth is at the center of our quest for the best that life can offer.

Most people seek to build their own sense of self-worth in three basic ways. Since people are often unaware of why they do what they do, let us take a closer look at these three ways. We will examine each approach and evaluate its usefulness for building self-worth and achieving our goals for life.

Self-worth strategy #1: What you have (the possessions approach)

One of the ways that people seek to build self-worth is through the accumulation of possessions. These are yesterday's "Yuppies" (young, upwardly-mobile professionals). They seek value in terms of the things they own, use, and display. If you ask possession-oriented people what they are worth, you might get an answer like this: "Oh, something around $450,000 in stocks, bonds, bank accounts, and real estate" (what some people in the financial world call the "bottom line"). Such people value themselves in terms of how much they have. It reminds me of the bumper sticker, "He Who Dies With the Most Toys Wins." That's a crass statement of the bottom-line approach to self-esteem.

I once had the privilege of receiving a BMW by mistake from a rental company in Frankfurt, Germany. Without speed limits on the German autobahns, I felt like I was in driver's heaven! Over the next two weeks, it became obvious why people love their BMWs—they make fantastic toys. Although I may never own one, I'll never forget the experience! Cynics say, "The only difference between the men and the boys is the price of their toys!" And although I am now past fifty years of age, I find there is no shortage of "toys" that still appeal to me and to my friends.

More and more, people's ideas about the meaning and value of life are shaped by movies and television shows. Have you noticed that a high percentage of the story lines coming out of Hollywood these days concerns heroes who go from rags to riches? In the past it was common for story lines to highlight a rich person giving up the perks of riches to identify with the poor, even at the risk of being misunderstood. But today it seems that no matter how poor the hero is, sooner or later in the story he is rewarded with riches and acclaim. These film and TV stories are very influential on young minds. As a result, many of today's young people identify riches with success and happiness.

I remember a young person like that. After graduating from college, I went back to the same inner-city school that I had attended—this time to teach. Chester was one of the students in my classes. He was a big, tough street kid from a devastated inner-city neighborhood. One day I asked Chester what he thought happiness was all about. He didn't hesitate one bit. "Happiness," he told me, "is a big, black, Cad–ee–llac." Is it really? To him it was. After all, in his neighborhood, the only people with money and respect seemed to be the pimps and the drug dealers who drove around in shiny black Cadillacs. To him, at that time, those cars represented everything that a person could want in this life. The "success" that these criminals exhibited outweighed any concern Chester might have had for the way in which they got wealthy.

Have you seen the bumper-sticker, "When Things Get Tough, the Tough Go Shopping!"? There is truth in that statement. When life gets difficult, shopping can provide a wonderful distraction. It can also provide the genuine satisfaction that comes from buying the latest and the greatest. It's a great feeling to bring home a fine sound system or TV and show it off to your friends. It's a great feeling to climb into a brand-new car and breathe in that great new-car smell. It's a great feeling to finally have the kind of home you always dreamed of, or even to add a nice sun-room to the basic home you've lived in for years. "Keeping up with the Joneses" is more than just a hobby. For many of us, it's about life, it's about being somebody, it's about what you are worth as a human being. Our possessions *can* have a major impact on how we feel about ourselves.

When the bottom drops out!

But there are some problems with the bottom-line approach to self-esteem. For one thing, toys don't last. They get scratched; they rot, rust, and crash—or, even worse, BMW comes out with a better car next year! Have you ever had a new car and decided to head out for a drive on a beautiful, sunny day? As you approached your car the sun shone off the paint at *just* the right angle, and you saw it—the first scratch! It can feel as if someone stuck a knife in your chest and twisted it. At such moments we realize that our possessions are more to us than just tools for life. They can represent some of our deepest needs and desires. And they *do* satisfy, at least for a while. In the end, however, the bottom-line approach is devastating to our self-worth because the feeling doesn't last. When the toy is broken, the joy of the toy is also gone.

Simple solution, you say? Just get so rich that you can have all the new toys you want all the time! After all, if you have a whole collection of BMWs, it won't matter if one of them gets scratched. If you have three hundred pairs of shoes, it won't matter if the heel comes off of one or two of them. If you can afford the ultimate palace, you will *know* that you are somebody.

But here is where a cruel deception seems to set in. The poor can always dream of getting rich and think that it will make a difference. But the rich soon discover that the more stuff they have, the less any of it is worth to them. They are blind-sided by a horrible side effect of wealth that I call "devaluation." Possessions lose value as they increase in quantity. There is something special about working and saving and dreaming about a purchase. The ultra-rich never get to experience this special pleasure. When you can have anything you want, whenever you want, it just doesn't mean all that much anymore. When someone spends $300 million on a single yacht or builds a home with more rooms than anyone could ever hope to use, doesn't this portray a certain sense of despair?

When my daughter, Tammy, was seven, she asked me, "Why does Oma (a German title for "Grandmother") always do things for other people and doesn't buy lots of things for herself?"

I told her, "Oma has learned that it is more blessed to give than to receive."

Tammy responded, "I don't understand that; I like getting presents and having lots of toys."

What does a daddy say to that? I remember telling her something like this: "Tammy, no child with a hundred toys can appreciate a toy the way a child can who has only one toy."

She thought for a moment, and then her eyes lit up. "You know what? That's true! I have so many toys that I don't even care about most of them anymore."

Smart kid. The problem with lots and lots of toys is that they become cheapened—devalued—with quantity. The problem with possessions is that the more you have, the less any of it means to you. It's a built-in, self-defeating mechanism. The poor may not have had a chance to discover it, but the rich know it well.

With plenty of possessions, you not only experience devaluation, but also worry. The more you have, the more you have to worry about—thieves, the financial markets, the motives of people who seek to be your friend. You may even worry more about your health, because wealth without health is nothing! And even if you succeed in being healthy and wealthy your whole life, you will eventually face the dilemma of the Pharaohs. You can't take it with you! No matter what your economic status in life, self-worth has to be built on something more permanent and more reliable than possessions.

Self-worth strategy #2: What you do (the self-development approach)

The second way that people seek to build self-worth is the self-development approach. They become performance-oriented. Performance-oriented people measure their worth in terms of how well they do certain things. They dream of accomplishing great things with their lives and then basking in the satisfaction that comes from achievement. They dream of becoming a star in the sports world. "If only I could be Brett Favre (the best quarterback in all of football right now), *then* I'd be somebody!" "If only I could be Michael Jordan or Tiger Woods, *then* I'd *really* be somebody." Young men, in particular, often gravitate toward bodybuilding or athletics as a way to build self-esteem. Work really hard at it, and you can become the big, tough guy you've always wanted to be! Women may search for the perfect body in a different way than do most men. They may focus on finding the right kind of makeup or the perfect dress that will make everybody's head turn.

Some people may be more interested in achievements of the mind than in achievements of the body. "I think I'll go back to school and get a Ph.D.; *then* I'll really be somebody." Perhaps we strive to be the best student in the class, the most successful salesperson on the team, the best-selling author in some topic, or even the best pastor in our area.

Others are drawn to the power and influence that can come from a position of prestige. "If only I could be president of the United States, *then* I'd really be somebody." Most of us would settle for being president of *anything!* Even a small corporation would do. For people in a religious context, being president of some church organization would be even better than being president of a company. If we never get that far, it would be great to own our own business at least, or be a recognized professional such as a lawyer, doctor, teacher, or preacher. In fact, some are tempted to become preachers because it puts them up front, in a position of some power and influence. In seeking a sense of self-worth, it's tempting to start valuing ourselves in terms of how much we've achieved in life. And, of course, there is a God-given sense of satisfaction that comes from accomplishing a task well, regardless of whether or not others recognize what we have done.

When achievement falls short

The self-development approach to self-worth, however, has some of the same problems as the bottom-line approach. Those who have achieved great things usually come to realize that the value of achievement in the pursuit of self-worth isn't nearly as great as one might think. If a high level of education, for example, were the key to self-worth, Ph.D.s should be the happiest people on earth, but that is simply not the case. If being an athletic star were the key to self-worth, there wouldn't be problems with drugs or alcohol in professional sports. Achievement alone does not spell satisfaction in life.

A high level of performance seems to suffer from its own kind of devaluation also. For example, a few years ago I would get very excited about breaking a hundred on the golf course. Today I am usually disappointed to score ninety (in golf, lower scores are better). The greater our performance, the higher we have to raise the bar. It is as if we were programmed to be dissatisfied with our achievements.

But even if achievement *could* give us the sought-after sense of self-worth, the satisfaction that comes from achievement doesn't last. No matter how successful we may have been, eventually we age. The athlete's body begins to fall apart. The professor's mind begins to play strange tricks. We get fired from that dream job. Or perhaps injury and illness rob us of our talent.

Many people remember Joe Montana, the best football quarterback of an earlier generation. At the age of thirty-eight Joe moved from the San Francisco 49ers to the Kansas City Chiefs. He was still great. He was still moving the team up and down the field. But his body was starting to fall apart. He spent more than half of that season on the bench, nursing an assortment of ailments. At the close of the season he was forced to retire, even though he could still play the game as well as anyone.

Sadder still was the experience of a former conference president whom I highly respect. He went into the triennial constituency meeting full of plans for the next three years in that conference. But instead of spending the afternoon directing the meeting that would discuss those plans, he spent it cleaning out his desk back at the office! Even though it was church business, the devastation of rejection hit him hard. To the extent that our self-worth is based on achievement—even the good things we do for the Lord—we are leaning on a broken stick that can snap at any time. We can be at the top of our profession one day, and the next day we can be cleaning out our desk.

Let us suppose, however, that you are extremely successful at what you are doing right now. You have a strong sense of satisfaction in your achievements, and there is no hint of destruction in sight. Is it safe to base your self-worth on your performance when you are performing well? Can you really find lasting self-worth in performance even when you are at your best? Think about it. Even the best basketball players miss a game-deciding shot now and then. Even the best golfers sometimes miss a three-foot putt. If your sense of self-worth is based on your daily performance, you can be up one day and down the next.

How I know! During one of our slow-pitch softball seasons at Andrews University, I played third base on the Seminary softball team. As a rule, I wasn't particularly good or bad. But one day I made four errors! Even though I'm a grown man and have spent most of my life teaching and writing, I was depressed for four days. Stupid, isn't it? Or does this kind of thing happen to you, too? Was I somehow finding self-worth in my performance on a slow-pitch softball team? I have since decided that it is better to be a pitcher than a third baseman. Pitchers don't make fielding mistakes in softball. The balls come by fast, and you either get the ball in your glove by luck, and they say, "Great play," or it gets by you, and they say, "Well, it was hit too hard anyway." But at third base there is no mercy.

Even though I am fully aware of the self-worth principles I'm sharing in this chapter, time and time again, I find myself measuring my worth on the basis of performance. That was certainly part of the reason I cried when the Bible teacher spoke to me so roughly. I had failed to meet my own expectations. I had hoped to be so good at refereeing that no one could find fault. Instead I experienced a miserable humiliation. Basing our value on performance and achievement is at best a fragile remedy for the human condition.

Self-worth strategy #3: Whom you know (the relationship approach)

The third way that people evaluate their worth as human beings is by the opinions others have of them and the way others behave toward them. In the first two approaches to self-worth, possessions and performance were the criteria. Now we turn to a relationship approach, in which the basis for how we feel about ourselves is our perception of what other people think of us. Their words, their behavior towards us, and our reactions to their words and behavior strongly affect our sense of self-worth if we are relationship-oriented individuals.

Of the three approaches to promoting self-worth that we have looked at so far, the relationship approach is the one we are most comfortable talking about. We generally feel more justified in building our self-worth on relationships than on possessions or performance. It certainly seems a bit nobler. Most of us don't want to be perceived as dependent on possessions or performance (although we all tend to be at one time or another), but we are willing to look to good relationships to provide a sufficient level of meaning and fulfillment in life. And experience certainly seems to suggest that relationships may be the answer we have been looking for.

A good illustration is teen romance. No doubt you've noticed the tremendous transformation in teenagers' lives when they discover that another human being out there thinks they are the beginning and end of all existence. Such a discovery suddenly changes everything! Thorns become roses in a miraculous transformation. Ugly ducklings become beautiful swans. Dull or negative personalities become radiant. Nothing has such tremendous power to boost our sense of value as the realization that another human being considers us precious, unique, and capable. Who we are, as human beings, is powerfully affected by what other people think.

Parents sometimes seek to find value in the lives and actions of their children. We want our kids to have opportunities that were not possible for us. We want them to succeed where we failed. We want them to be all that they can be. In the process, we sometimes place on our kids the tremendous burden of carrying our values as well as their own. When they perform well or succeed at a task, we take pride in that *ourselves*. When they fail or are rejected by their peers, we take that personally as well. What other people think of us has a powerful effect on our sense of self-worth. What others think of those we love can have a similar effect.

The people-oriented approach also explains the power of celebrities in today's world. When I was a teenager, my brother suggested that we attend a political rally. It was 1964, and Barry Goldwater was running for president against Lyndon Johnson. Goldwater was scheduled to deliver a speech that evening at an airplane hangar about a mile from our home. My brother thought it would be fun to go and hear what he had to say.

After parking my brother's car at the nearby airport, we approached the airplane hangar. Just before we arrived at the main door, it suddenly burst open, and three girls in red, white, and blue Republican hats came running out. They were screaming, "I'll never wash it again. I'll never wash it again. He shook my hand. I'll never wash it again!" They had apparently been given an opportunity to meet the candidate privately before the speech. I've thought about those girls ever since. I have wondered what their hands look like after more than thirty-five years! It's amazing how contact with a celebrity can affect our sense of who we are and what we are worth. Close contact with someone who seems to be somebody can offer a tremendous boost to our self-esteem.

That is the main reason people practice "name dropping." When someone hints casually that he or she is a personal friend of (or even related to) some famous person, it implies added value for that person. You will no doubt be impressed to hear that I am related to Hillary Clinton. Such relationships can, of course, provide special access to a public person. I remember one of the times when the Clintons were going through some tremendous difficulties with public accusations of infidelity. I thought that Hillary would appreciate some ministerial advice on how to deal with that difficult situation. I explained to her some of the dynamics of Bill's childhood that affect the way he relates to the women around him. I walked her through some tools and strategies that spouses can use to cope with the tragedy of infidelity. I offered encouragement that God would be with her no matter what took place.

I actually did say these things to her. She and Bill were attending a rally at the Hoosier Dome in Indianapolis, Indiana. I was driving by the Dome on the interstate highway that passes nearby. I really did tell her about these things—while driving by. Somehow, I'm not sure she heard me. . . . Oh, by the way, not only am I related to Hillary, I am also related to Bill. I'm not exactly sure *how* we are related, but the Bible conclusively demonstrates that all three of us go back to Adam and Eve!

When I use this illustration in public presentations, the place immediately goes quiet and eyes widen slightly as people hear of my being related to Hillary. I can see them drinking in the implications. I can sense that the audience is increasingly impressed with my importance. But are they mad at me afterward for tricking them! Nothing that I wrote above is false, it is the impression I leave that demonstrates the power of name dropping. Why are we so strongly tempted to exaggerate our connections with important people? Because the higher a person's social status is, the more value their opinion of us has in the eyes of others. We measure our value by what others think of us. Although the Clintons are not universally admired, their constant presence in the public eye during the '90s give their personalities great evocative power in the minds of everyday people.

The above discussion underlines a major reality. Human value is assigned by others. And the value of a human being far transcends what they are made of physically. I understand that the total value of the minerals and chemicals in the average human body is only about twelve dollars. But if you value that same body in biological terms, its various organs can be worth millions on the transplant market. Even more extravagant is the value of the human spirit. The personality of a Michael Jordan or a Tiger Woods is valued in hundreds of millions of dollars. And Americans value the ideas of a Bill Gates or a Warren Buffet in multiplied billions of dollars! But that is little encouragement to most of us when we feel rejected or set aside by others.

When people let you down

Although we often measure human value in terms of what others think of us, this process proves to be very fragile as a basis for self-worth. Looking to others for a sense of self-worth can be damaging both to them and us. Take marriage as an example, since marriage is the most common way that people seek to build self-worth through relationships. Many people enter into marriage in the fond hope that the value they have found in the eyes of another will carry them along throughout their married lives. People seek self-worth in marriage in two primary ways, and neither of them succeed in the long run.

1. The Takers: People who are quite needy hope to find worth in terms of what they receive from others. Their emotional and psychological needs generally motivate them to seek affirmation and support; they have little energy left over for nurturing others. From time to time they may feel good about building others up, but the predominant role for many people is the "takers" role.

2. The Givers: On the other hand, people who are more naturally secure may find much personal value in building up and nurturing others. They gain a sense of worth by giving more encouragement and help than they receive. Some "givers" enjoy being affirmed from time to time; others hate it. But in either case, for "givers," the predominant motivation in a relationship is the joy they receive from affirming and encouraging others.

Most human beings are a bit more complicated than these simple categories suggest. In fact, experience suggests that the vast majority of people are more "takers" than "givers," yet most people would argue that they are primarily "givers." There is a serious disconnection with reality here! So the approach I take in what follows may not resonate with everyone. It does show, however, that the search for self-worth through relationships is handicapped almost from the start no matter what the primary tendencies of the individuals in a given relationship may be.

1. The "taker-taker" marriage. A marriage between two "takers" can quickly create a hell that makes even loneliness seem attractive. The couple is like a pair of hungry lion cubs demanding more and more, with neither having the resources to provide what the other needs. The flowering of self-esteem that romance provided (the bloom of romance can make temporary "givers" out of "takers") is quickly transformed into the crushing disappointment of conflict and unfulfilled needs. Two empty people looking to each other in order to be filled—that is the formula for a major disaster. Marriage between "takers" is common—after all there are more "takers" in the world than "givers," but it is not the most common marriage bond.

2. The "giver-taker" marriage. More often than not, as implausible as it may sound, "givers" and "takers" are attracted to each other. To them, the arrangement can seem like a marriage made in heaven. "Givers" need to give, and "takers" need to take. So why not link them up so everyone can be happy? But this, too, is a formula for disaster. In extreme cases in which there are highly committed "givers" and "takers" in a marriage, the "taker" never has to grow up. He can just go on playing his video games, watching football, and goofing off with his friends, while his surrogate "mother" takes care of the kids as well as him and struggles, in between, to find money to pay the bills (of course, the female can also be the "taker" in such a marriage).

The "giver-taker" marriage is destructive to the "takers" in that they are locked into a dependency that prevents them from discovering the fulfillment that comes with personal growth and investment in the growth of others. The "takers" will not gain the skills needed to achieve their hopes and dreams in life. And no "giver" could ever give enough to satisfy a "taker's" endless need for affirmation and support. So the "giver-taker" marriage that began with so much hope ends by shattering all hope for a genuine sense of value and purpose in life.

Life's Bottom Line

The "giver-taker" relationship is destructive to the "giver" as well. To the extent that giving is the *basis* for self-worth rather than the *result*, giving becomes a dead-end street, no matter how noble it may appear at first glance. The "giver" in such a marriage quickly discovers that very little affirmation and support is coming back in return. A conscientious "giver" suspects that her giving is inadequate and redoubles her efforts. But lack of support, in return, eventually leads to a number of unhealthy responses. The "giver" may burn out or break down as a result of overwhelming outflow with nothing coming back in return. The "giver" may use the giving to manipulate responses from the "taker," which "takers" usually find even more galling than neglect. The "giver" eventually loses respect for the "taker," leading to a serious breakdown in the relationship.

3. The "giver-giver" marriage. The secret to self-worth, then, would seem to be found in a "giver-giver" relationship. But let's examine this possibility a bit more closely. For starters, a "giver-giver" marriage is truly rare indeed. "Givers" tend not to be attracted to each other in part because many "givers" feel uncomfortable with other "givers." When your sense of self-worth is dependent on giving, receiving from another produces guilt and embarrassment. The reluctance of both parties to take frustrates each in their attempts to obtain self-esteem through the relationship. "Takers" are much more attractive since they meet the "giver's" need to give and find value in giving. Marriages between "givers" tend to break up when one or the other finds himself or herself fascinated with some deeply needy soul "out there." Even the "ideal" marriage in human terms, then, is not the ultimate answer to our human need for worth and meaning in life.

The same goes for our tendency to seek personal value through our children or through interaction with the "celebrities" that may cross our path. When a person seeks self-worth in children or grandchildren, it places incredible pressure on a young person. Children are forced to meet needs in their parents that they were never designed to meet. Parents seeking to fulfill their needs in their children tend to be very hard on their kids, holding them to impossibly high expectations. Too often such parents come home one day to find a note that says, "I know that no matter what I do it will never be good

25

enough for you. I decided, therefore, to put an end to our misery (or run away)."

Seeking value through celebrities also falls short. That famous Hollywood star is usually just as empty of self-worth as anyone—often more so. Many celebrities are amazed and even confused that other people think so highly of them. The divorce rate in Hollywood gives clear evidence of their own struggles with self-worth. If being in a relationship with a Hollywood actor is the be all and end all of self-esteem, why do so many actors fail at marriage over and over again? Celebrities may smile on the screen, but when they get home they often can't stand the person they're living with or the life that they have to live.

Our dependence on celebrities can be destructive even to them. They become the ultimate "givers." A lot of praise and affirmation comes with being a star. But there is also the constant press of people with "needs" for celebrity affirmation. Constantly giving such affirmation through a word, an autograph, or a small piece of time can be draining. After a while, a celebrity comes to feel totally empty and lifeless from all the giving. And being a public person means public criticism on the part of at least some followers. As success raises expectations, criticism inevitably follows. And criticism hurts celebrities just as much as anyone else. The result? Far too many celebrities have ended their own lives or self-destructed on alcohol or drugs.

Even if we are fortunate enough to be in a healthy and mutually affirming relationship, the danger still remains that it may not last. The value that we gain through relationships with others tends to be temporary, fickle, and fleeting. Many times I have been excited to make a new friend only to discover that he or she is about to move halfway across the country. Professors can be reluctant to get close to graduate students because they almost always move away in a year or two. But even when the person that respects and admires you doesn't move away, there is always the chance that he may find out something about you that will change his mind.

Some know by experience how devastating divorce can be. You start with a person who has made a huge difference in your life. He thought the world of you and built you up in many ways. You found yourself depending on him for meaning and value. Then the day comes when, in the words of one divorcée, "he tore my heart out, threw it on the ground, stomped on it for a while, and then spat on it." What rejection or humiliation can top that? If you're depending on another human being for your sense of who you are, you're setting yourself up for disaster. When your best friend can betray you, whom can you trust?

Even in the best-case relationship, each of us is only a few breaths away from the reality of death. I'll never forget the time a lady called and said, "My husband just went and died on me!" She was angry! For forty-two years he had been the earth and sky to her. For forty-two years her sense of self-worth was grounded in the love he had for her. He had no right to die when she needed him so much! Do you sense what she was feeling? "This man was everything to me, and when he died it was as bad as if he'd gone off with someone else." Her anger was real and understandable.

While the approach to self-worth that focuses on others seems to hold some promise in special cases, in the end it proves just as ephemeral as the other two approaches.

Self-worth strategy #4: The ultimate relationship (an ideal partner)

Is there no way out? Are all human approaches to finding a sense of value doomed to end in disappointment? The answer to that question is both "Yes" and "No." You see, the ways that we seek to find self-esteem sometimes do more harm than good. One thing is for sure—the bottom-line approach is *not* the way. Anyone who has lots of things knows that things don't satisfy in any long-term sense. Just ask a Kennedy sometime. If money and the things it can provide were the basis for happiness, the Kennedys would be one of the happiest families on earth. One can have it all in the material sense, yet discover that it doesn't do the job.

Furthermore, people who have achieved know that achievement doesn't satisfy in any long-term sense either. Professional basketball players not only make millions of dollars a year, they are celebrities at the highest level. But if money and fame is where it is at, why are so many basketball stars seeking solace in alcohol, casual affairs, and drugs? Why turn to drugs when you are living the very life that so many others would love to live? Apparently, achievement, even when combined with extensive wealth, is not the path to happiness and fulfillment.

Is there no way out? The esteem of others seems to be the only hope left. But it appears that we cannot find a sense of value in a relationship with just anyone. It takes a friend with special characteristics to provide the kind of self-worth we so desperately need. As I see it, what we need is a friend with four unique characteristics.

1. Someone who has genuine, inherent value. What we need is a friend who is genuinely and inherently valuable. Not a Magic Johnson who is seeking fulfillment in the same dead-ends that you and I often pursue. It has to be someone who is inherently valuable. Someone who doesn't need to find value in others or in things. Someone who is worthwhile because of who he already is.

2. Someone who knows all about us. This friend should also be someone who knows all about us, because relationships filled with secrets and surprises are fragile relationships. You never know when people will find something out about you and change their minds. "Oh, if that's the way you really are, I don't want to have anything to do with you." The kind of relationship that builds self-worth doesn't keep secrets in a closet somewhere. Openness and transparency are critical.

3. Someone who loves us as we are. Many people, however, have decided that they don't like us on account of who we are. We need a genuine, true friend who is not fazed by our weaknesses and shortcomings. We need someone who has taken the time to know us intimately, yet is fully committed to accepting us and loving us no matter what we may say or do. We need someone who will never leave us even when we try to leave him. We need someone who knows all about us, yet loves us just the same. Such a relationship can provide a secure floor under our sense of self-worth.

4. Someone who will never die. Even a relationship with all three characteristics will be insecure as long as death looms as a daily threat. You could find the perfect partner who meets your self-worth demands, only to lose him in death just when you need him most. The ultimate problem with self-worth is that we will truly find it in a relationship only with a person who will live forever.

As hopeless as that sounds, let's consider for a moment the positive consequences of finding a friend who (1) is genuinely valuable, (2) knows all about us, (3) loves us just the same, and (4) will never die. To be loved and cherished by such a person will even out the ups and downs in our experience. As we're basking in that kind of love, we are freed from the need to prove ourselves to others (and even to ourselves); we can have an inner peace about who we are. If we are loved by someone who is truly valuable, it won't really matter anymore what others think about us. When somebody starts criticizing us and tearing us down, we can just smile to ourselves and say, "Consider the source. I already have the one relationship that truly matters. Ignore the distraction."

Genuine self-worth means that life offers a tremendous sense of fulfillment, knowing that we matter to the one person in our life who truly matters. Only when our own deepest needs are met, can we begin to truly consider other people's needs. Out of our sense of value we will be able to give ourselves in service to others without expecting or manipulating some return.

A true sense of self-worth is also the basis for genuine freedom. Possessions, performance, and people—as avenues to self-worth—confine us in slavery to an illusion. We strive mightily each day for things and experiences that do not satisfy in the ultimate sense. But when we know that God accepts us, we become alive to reality as it actually is. We become alive to our own weaknesses, yet without self-condemnation. We become alive to the needs of others, yet without the need to manipulate them for our own purposes. In Christ we escape from confinement in the "world" to a reality that transcends our limited experience. It is like the movie The *Truman Show* in which the main actor, without knowing it, has lived all his life in a giant motion picture set—all his interactions with others carefully programmed. At the end of the movie, Truman finds a door at the "horizon," and escapes from his made-up world into reality!

A sense of self-worth is truly the basis for a life that is worth living. But is it really possible on this earth? Is there anyone out there who is truly valuable and lives forever? Or are we simply talking in philosophical terms about something that will never happen to us? Have we truly reached the end of all hope? Is there no way out? No! No! A thousand times No! The greatest story ever told is that a Friend, with exactly the four characteristics described above, actually does exist. I'm talking about a Person who is worth the whole universe, who lives forever, who knows everything about you, and who loves you just the way you are. And He is eager to make Himself known to you.

The name of this Friend is Jesus. Is He truly valuable? The reality is that He made the whole universe and everything that is in it. He's worth the whole universe and any universe that could ever be created. He owns more and has achieved more than anyone else we could imagine. Does He know all about us? Yes, He does, even our innermost thoughts and feelings (see John 2:23-25; Hebrews 4:12, 13). Does He love us in spite of all He knows about us? Yes, He does; He loves you and me so much that He would have died for us if we had been the only ones who needed saving! He died for us even before we did anything to respond to Him (see Romans 5:6, 8). And now that He has been raised from the dead, death has no more claim on Him (see 1 Corinthians 15).

Jesus meets all the qualifications of the one we need so desperately. He is the kind of friend who offers real hope. You don't have to deserve Jesus; you don't have to earn His love. He already loves and accepts you as you are. It doesn't matter what you've done or where you've been. He is the one true Source of self-worth. If we're looking for self-esteem anywhere else, we will find it only for a time, and then we will lose it again. That's reality. But our situation is not hopeless. Our truest and most valuable Friend lives, and His name is Jesus.

To me, this explains the tremendous survival of Christianity. Century after century, Christianity goes on, because century after century people discover what it means to know Jesus. They discover that knowing Him is the key to everything that matters in life. This explains the martyrs. Would people go to death for Jesus unless they knew that dying with Jesus was preferable to living without Him?

This is why the assurance of salvation, of being right with God, is not optional. Human beings desperately need to know where they stand in the universe, what they are truly worth. If you don't know that you have eternal life, that you are right with God, you will be forced to seek that reality in some other way. You will live by the bottom line, by your performance, or you will depend on your human relationships for happiness. You may even seek life through religious achievements and relationships.

But none of these will truly satisfy. More often than not, people without the assurance of salvation become critical and faultfinding. Without even realizing it, they have turned away from Jesus to seek life in possessions, performance, or people. Assurance of salvation, on the other hand, is the basis for radiant, joyful living. When you know that you are right with God, you don't have to prove yourself to Him or to anyone else. You don't have to accumulate things, trophies, or relationships.

Assurance of salvation is also the key to turning away from sin. Sin is simply a dead-end approach for meeting your own personal needs. Sin is trying to meet your needs by buying things. Sin is trying to meet your needs by performance or in another person. At times, even pastors may come to a point in their lives when they say, "My life is empty, and maybe this other person can provide the spark I need. Maybe this other person will love me the way I deserve to be loved." And that person is not your spouse. Sin is anything, even a good thing, that promises life apart from a relationship with Jesus. A comfortable home is a good thing. Successful evangelistic campaigns and academic degrees are good things. Solid relationships with other human beings are good things. But if any of these take the place of Jesus in our lives, they will prove to be false hopes.

This is what temptation is all about. Temptation is not simply an urge to do something evil or contrary to the laws of God or humanity. Temptation is often an urge to do something good *in order to* find life. Even the best of activities can become substitutes for real life. So whenever we are tempted by these three areas of self-esteem—performance, possessions, or people—we need to ask ourselves some serious questions.

Why is my need not being met in Christ right now? Why am I really buying these toys? Why do I think I need to go back to school? Why am I trying to find a better job? Why am I wanting to develop this particular relationship? Why is this person so attractive to me?

We tend to avoid reflecting on such questions. But reasons matter. The bottom line is this: unless our sense of worth is established in our relationship with Jesus Christ, we will be forced to seek it somewhere else, and the results will not be pretty.

Biblical or psychological?

Are these concepts truly biblical or have I gotten lost in the mazes of psychology? This is a very important question. Unless our basic answers to life are grounded in more than just human assumptions, we are simply headed for disappointment. Fortunately, the Bible *does* speak strongly to the issue of self-worth. The key word that leads us into the biblical perspective on value is the word "glory." The crucial question the Bible writers ask is this: "What do you glory in?" Let's look at a few texts in closing.

Jeremiah 9:23, 24 (NKJ) says:

> "Let not the wise man glory in his wisdom,
> Let not the strong man glory in his strength,
> Nor let the rich man glory in his riches;
> But let the one who glories glory in this:
> That he understands and knows me."

Possessions

Jeremiah says, "Don't glory in riches, in possessions. Don't glory in physical or mental strength. Glory in the Lord—that's what life is all about." Jeremiah saw clearly that the basis of real life could not be found in our fascination with possessions and performance. John 12:42, 43 points us to the perils of people-oriented glory:

People

> Many of the rulers believed in Him,
> but they did not confess it on account of the Pharisees,
> in order that they might not be thrown out of the synagogue:
> For they loved the glory of men
> more than the glory of God.

Why did the rulers of the time reject Jesus? Because they loved the praise that other people provided more than the praise that God provides. Whenever we place human relationships ahead of God, we show what we truly value in life.

Perhaps the best text dealing with the subject of self-worth and its substitutes is found in Galatians 6:14.

> May I never ever glory,
> except in the cross of our Lord Jesus Christ,
> through whom the world has been crucified to me,
> and I to the world.

When Paul talks in this text about "the world," he is talking about possessions, performance, and people. That's what the "world" is all about. The world is necessary; we could not exist without possessions, achievements, and relationships with other people. But even the best things of this world cannot compete with the Cross as a means for determining human value. Nothing that I do, or that anyone else does for me, could possibly take the place of what God has done for me in Jesus Christ.

When we truly know what the Cross means, we will have something to glory about. When we truly understand the significance of what Christ has done for us on the cross, the world with its possessions, performance, and people will find its true place. The Cross tells us that the greatest Person in the whole universe valued us so much that He was willing to die for us. That places infinite value upon us. To Jesus, we are worth as much as the whole universe. Possessions, performance, and people are important, but their role in building self-worth is insignificant in comparison with the Cross. When we depend upon possessions, performance, and people for our sense of value, these things become sin, dead-end ways to finding self-worth.

For the Bible, then, one question looms above all others regarding what human beings are worth. The question that the Bible asks us about self-esteem is this: "Where is your glory?" Is your greatest glory in possessions, performance, or a list of friends? Or do you glory in the cross of Jesus Christ? Where is your glory? That becomes the ultimate question.

the ultimate / question !

CHAPTER

2

BATTING 1.000 IN THE GAME OF LIFE

In chapter one we learned that the only way to a genuine sense of self-worth is through a relationship with Jesus. All other substitutes for a sense of value will not satisfy in the long run. And it is only through such a sense of value that we can become the kind of people we need to be and want to be.

This leaves us with the crucial question: How can we have that kind of relationship with Jesus? How can we come into an acceptable standing before God? How can we know when we are right with God? What must we do in order to have eternal life? (see Matthew 19:16). From a human perspective, the obvious answer is: Make no mistakes! Live an irreproachable life. Live fault-free. Then God will *have* to accept us! But as logical as this approach may seem, it has serious problems. In this chapter we will take another look at one of the clearest texts on this subject in the Bible. Unless the gospel, the "good news," that we believe and share is solidly grounded in God's revelation, we may find ourselves falling back into traps of illusion. And we cannot expect secular people to give up their illusions for something even less certain! So let's take a fresh look at what the Bible calls "salvation."

Make no mistakes!

The Christian life is a lot like baseball—at least that has been true in my experience. We often get up in the morning, determined to bat a thousand for the day. (For those readers who may be intellectually challenged where baseball is concerned, batting 1.000 [pronounced "a thousand"] means hitting the ball safely every time you come to bat—something that rarely happens in a single game, much less over a season or a player's career.) We may think to ourselves, "Today I'm going to be really nice to the spouse and patient with the kids. Today I'm going to think only nice thoughts about the boss." If it is Sabbath, we plan to think about amazing grace only and never about Mark Grace (a well-known Chicago Cubs baseball player).

Then evening comes, and we realize that we have fallen way short of our intentions again. So we begin to beat up on ourselves. We start saying things like, "What difference does it make to be a Christian after all? Am I never going to change?"

No wonder there are so many long-faced Christians! How could anyone possibly rejoice in the context of continual failure and frustration? I mean, life is a real battle. I can understand Christians who feel they have no time to smile, no time to celebrate. I can understand such Christians because that is my battle, too. I am battling, and I get bruised every day. I haven't hit a thousand yet, either.

One Sabbath, however, I was determined to do it. I got up long before the rest of the family. I spent an hour in devotions, got myself prepared for Sabbath, had my multi-grain breakfast cereal, and gently awakened the family so that my wife could take care of her own needs. Then I got the kids washed, dressed, and fed. We made it to Sabbath School on time without a single word of frustration. I was feeling really good that Sabbath morning—until little Kimberly's Sabbath School teacher came up to me and said, "You dressed Kimberly this morning, didn't you?"

"Yes, I did," I answered with just a touch of pride. I thought she would think, "Wow, what a man!"

But instead she looked me in the eye and said, "She has her shoes on backwards" (left for right)!

So much for batting a thousand that Sabbath day! It may seem trivial, but the reversal of shoes triggered in me all the sense of

[handwritten margin note: Illus: shoes on backward]

failure that a more serious infraction would have.

Paul and baseball—a two-fold problem

In the book of Romans, Paul summed up the deeper picture of our human existence. He never played baseball, but he seems to have understood exactly what I am talking about. In Romans 3:23 he described the fundamental problem of human life in a few short words:

> For all have sinned
> and fall short of the glory of God.

If you follow baseball at all, you know that no one ever bats 1.000 for more than a game or two. Actually, most players feel really good if they bat as high as .300 (pronounced "three hundred") over the course of a season. Mark Grace is currently one of the better baseball hitters. For his entire career he has batted around .315. That means that he succeeds in batting safely about 30 percent of the time and fails about 70 percent of the time. The most successful hitter of all time was Ty Cobb; he batted .367 over the length of his career. So even Ty Cobb failed nearly twice as often as he succeeded.

What Paul tells us in Romans 3:23 underlines the point that life is a lot like baseball. Just as even the best baseball players succeed only occasionally in the midst of general failure, so Paul indicts all humanity when he says, "All have sinned." Grammatically, the Greek word Paul uses for "sinned" is an *aorist indicative*, which, in this sentence, expresses the idea that sin is characteristic of our entire past history seen as a whole. We all have a past record that we wish did not exist. Every one of us has made plenty of "outs" in the course of our career. There are no exceptions to this rule outside of Jesus Himself. This is why "every human mouth needs to be closed and the whole world made accountable to God" (Romans 3:19). This is why the "works of the law" cannot be the basis for anyone to get right with God (see Romans 3:20). Everyone has made sufficient mistakes to come under the law's condemnation. Batting a perfect 1.000 is the requirement, and no one has ever met that requirement. Anyone who has reached adulthood has made enough mistakes to be forever doomed in the eyes of the law.

But the problem is far more serious even than this. Even if our past record could somehow be forgiven, it still wouldn't be enough. Paul goes on to say that we all "fall short of the glory of God" (Romans 3:23). This means that even if we could get a fresh start, our best deeds from then on wouldn't be good enough to meet the standard. The Greek word Paul uses for "fall short" is a *present continuous* tense. This emphasizes the continuous nature of our falling short. The inadequacy of even the good things we do is ongoing and constant. All of us continually fall short of the glory of God. Paul makes it clear that, just like baseball players who bat .200, .300, or even .400, our best efforts fall far short of the ideal. Every one of us continually fails to bat 1.000 in the Christian life; we all continually fall short of the glory of God.

Now it may seem unreasonable of God to expect that human beings somehow live up to His standards of character. After all, He is God, and we are humans. But I believe that Paul's point here is a practical one. He is affirming what we already sense deep inside. With few exceptions, most of us sense that we are not living up to our own standards of right and wrong, much less God's! How do I know? Whenever we criticize others, we are raising the bar for our own performance. If we think a thought or action is wrong in another, we sense that it is equally wrong in ourselves as well. Paul is helping us avoid a false sense of self-worth, one based on an inadequate concept of human responsibility.

In Romans 3:23, then, Paul identifies two realities in our lives that make it impossible for us to be saved on the basis of our own efforts. First, we all have a past record of sinful thoughts and acts that we cannot take back. At some time, we all have rebelled against God; we all have done things that reflect our natural enmity against Him (see Romans 8:7). Second, even our best efforts in the present, even our good deeds, fall short of the ideal that God has held out before us. We have failed—not only in keeping His Ten Commandment law, but also in following the perfect example of Jesus' earthly life. If, therefore, I am counting on my *performance* as the basis for getting right with God, my situation is hopeless (see Romans 1:18-3:20), and so is that of all humanity. There has to be some other way to attain God's favor and enter into a relationship with Him.

And, thank God, there is.

Being justified before God

Paul doesn't waste my time getting right to the solution. He summarizes it simply and clearly in Romans 3:24 where he tells us how God treats people who have sinned in the past and who continually fall short of His glory in the present:

> Being justified freely by his grace
> through the redemption which is in Christ Jesus.

When Paul speaks of "being justified," he is concerned with how a person fares under God's scrutiny in the final judgment at the end of history (see Romans 2:12, 13; 3:6, 19, 20). In that context the connection between verses 23 and 24 is startling. In fact, it is so startling that some biblical scholars suggest that verse 23 was not original with Paul, but must have been added later by an editor who misunderstood him. The biblical message sometimes seems too good to be true. But since there is no evidence that anyone has tampered with this text, we must assume that verses 23 and 24 express the message that Paul intended.

Speaking of those who "have sinned and continually fall short of the glory of God," Paul describes them as "being justified." "Being justified" is a *present participle* in the original language. According to basic Greek grammars, the time of a participle is understood as being relative to the time of the main verb. In this case, the main verbs are "have sinned" and "fall short." The action of a present participle occurs at the same time as the main verb. Grammatically, what this all means is that we "are being justified" not only in relation to the sins we have done in the past, but also in relation to the sins we commit as we continually fall short in the present! This is incredibly good news!

The sin problem is a two-fold one, therefore, the solution must also be a two-fold one. We all have a sorry record that needs to be forgiven. We all are also daily doing things that fall short of the glory of God. Justification solves both problems. It covers our sins of the *past*, and it also covers our falling short in the *present*. In Romans 4, Paul describes these two aspects of justification further. To those, like David, who have done terrible sins, God offers forgiveness (see Romans 4:6-8). To those, like Abraham, who have done plenty of good things, but who are still short of the mark, there comes an accounting of righteousness from God (see Romans 4:1-5). I would illustrate the two-fold nature of this justification as follows:

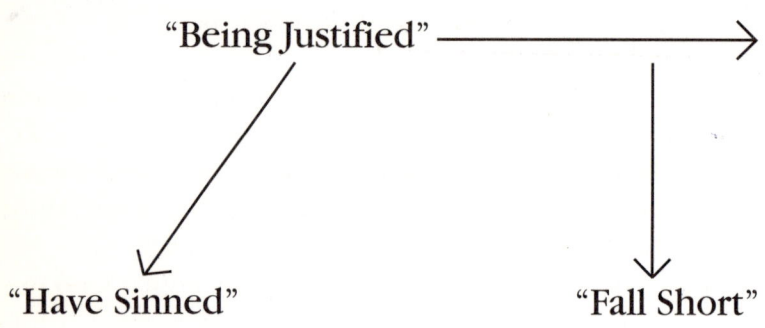

The "being justified" of Romans 3:24 indicates that God looks back on the sinful record of our past and forgives it. But the justification that Paul speaks about is not merely a one-time act on God's part that leaves us to our own devices from then on. The "being justified" remains in place as a continual upgrading of our best efforts. "Justification" not only forgives the record of the past, it also makes up the difference between our best efforts and God's high and holy standards. We stand right with God, therefore, not just for the moment when we are forgiven, but continually through the ongoing imputation of His righteousness to our daily actions. What good news! Our standing with God is not subject to the ups and downs of our daily obedience, but to the ongoing nature of His perfect righteousness!

Batting 1.000 in the Game of Life

To readers from an Adventist background this may sound startling or new. So let me share a few statements from Ellen White that show that this view of getting right with God is not a new one to Seventh-day Adventist thought. The first statement deals with the inadequacy of even our good deeds for pleasing God:

> The religious services, the prayers, the praise, the penitent confession of sin ascend from true believers as incense to the heavenly sanctuary, but passing through the corrupt channels of humanity, they are so defiled that unless purified by blood, they can never be of value with God. They ascend not in spotless purity, and unless the Intercessor, who is at God's right hand, presents and purifies all by His righteousness, it is not acceptable to God....
>
> Oh, that all may see that everything in obedience, in penitence, in praise and thanksgiving, must be placed upon the glowing fire of the righteousness of Christ" (*Selected Messages*, vol. 1, p. 344).

Even the finest and most God-honoring actions that we can conceive (obedience, praise, prayer) need the addition of Christ's perfect righteousness in order to be acceptable to God. Even in our worship we continually fall short of the glory of God.

The next statement underlines the fact that our completeness comes only in Christ.

> When it is in the heart to obey God, when efforts are put forth to this end, Jesus accepts this disposition and effort as man's best service, and He makes up for the deficiency with His own divine merit (*Selected Messages*, vol. 1, p. 382).

A similar statement follows:

> The soul who sees Jesus by faith, repudiates his own righteousness. He sees himself as incomplete, his repentance insufficient, his strongest faith but feebleness, his most

costly sacrifice as meager, and he sinks in humility at the foot of the cross. But a voice speaks to him from the oracles of God's Word. In amazement he hears the message, "Ye are complete in Him." Now all is at rest in his soul (*Faith and Works*, pp. 107, 108).

Ellen White rightly emphasized the importance of obedience as a response to the mighty work of God in our lives. But these statements make it clear that such obedience can *never* be the basis upon which we become acceptable to God. The decisive work of salvation must come from outside of us. Ellen White and Paul are not in contradiction to each other.

Let's get back to Romans 3. On what basis can God justify those who have sinned and continually fall short of His glory? How can He justify the ungodly (see Romans 4:5) without going contrary to His own character? How can God acquit messed-up people in the final judgment of earth's history? Paul summarizes God's strategy for justifying sinners in three parts. We are being justified by grace, in Jesus Christ and through faith. Notice what the text says:

> For all have sinned
> and fall short of the glory of God,
> Being justified freely *by His grace*
> through the redemption which is *in Christ Jesus:*
> Whom God set forth as a sacrificial atonement
> *through faith* in his blood.... (Romans 3:23-25).

By grace

The first part of the divine strategy that Paul is laying out in Romans 3 is that we're saved by grace, "freely." The Greek word translated "freely" is found also in John 15:25. There Jesus says, "They hated me *without a cause.*" The phrase "without a cause" translates the exact same Greek word that is translated "freely" in Romans 3:24. Jesus was hated without a cause. In other words, He did absolutely nothing to deserve people's hate. Similarly, our justification is "without a cause." We have done absolutely nothing to deserve being justified. We are justified "without a cause" by His grace.

In the original language, the word "grace" is related to the word "gift." How much do you have to do to earn a gift? If it is a gift, you don't do anything. It is given freely, without a cause, sometimes for no reason but that the person likes you or cares about you. In other words, grace is a quality that is in God's heart, not ours. No amount of believing, obeying, repenting, or obeying on our part causes God to regard us as just or righteous. His grace itself is the reason for showering His salvation upon us. And that grace isn't a one-time act. We are "being justified" without a cause by His grace. The grace is as continual as is the justification. As continual as is our falling short of the glory of God!

This means that throughout our life we stand justified freely by grace. Are you glad? I certainly am! Every day I recognize that I am a fallible human being. That in spite of my best efforts, I am a person who doesn't live up to my own standards, much less those of others. My intentions can all be in the right direction, but when the end of the day comes, I have not batted 1.000 that day, and I know it. So when I kneel down at the side of my bed, I thank God that the Bible makes it clear that I am justified freely by God's grace—continually. Grace is not about something that I have done, but about something that God has chosen to shower upon me. Ellen White used the term "unmerited favor" as a definition for grace. In other words, I did nothing to deserve God's favor. God looks upon us favorably without our even deserving it. That is what grace is all about.

But the news about grace gets even better. This continual grace lasts a long, long time. All the way to the Second Coming. The next time you look at the book *The Great Controversy*, check out page 641 where Ellen White describes Jesus Christ coming in the clouds. God's people are looking up and seeing Him coming. What are they saying as Jesus approaches on the clouds? Are they saying, "Well it's about time! I've been batting 1.000 now for the last twenty-five years, so I know I'm ready!"? Absolutely not. As Jesus approaches, the last thing on their minds is their own readiness to meet Him! Instead they cry out, "Who shall be able to stand?" These are the people of God, not the wicked ones who have just cried for the rocks and mountains to fall on them. Even the righteous at the time of the Second Coming will feel unworthy to live in the presence of God's incredible glory. What does Jesus say to them? " 'My grace is sufficient for you' " (2 Corinthians 12:9). At the Second Coming!

Dear reader, if we can rejoice in His grace at the Second Coming, do you think it might be alright to do a little bit of rejoicing today? Might we even be able to smile now and then—even on days when we bat, say .148, like I do sometimes? Jesus says, "My grace is sufficient for you." To me, this is absolutely fantastic! And this grace is not only sufficient, it is bestowed without a cause. I have everything I need because God cared enough to give it to me. I don't deserve it, and in some sense I will never deserve it, but God bestows it without a cause.

So Paul opens his discussion of the grounds of our salvation with the assertion that it is by grace. But Paul doesn't stop with this first step. If Paul had stopped here, he would have left the impression that God is like an indulgent parent. And to be honest with you, I don't particularly care for indulgent parents.

I remember being in a grocery store and seeing a little kid knocking things down from the shelves, getting in the way, and making all kinds of mess and trouble. I was starting to grit my teeth in frustration when I saw his mom come along. But instead of taking control of the situation, she just smiled at me and said, "Oh, isn't he cute?" Well, I didn't think he was cute. And I wondered what kind of adult he would become as a result of that kind of parenting. That mother was sending her kid the message that it doesn't matter what you do—follow your heart, everything that comes natural is OK. And we know the destructive consequences of that kind of parenting style.

In Christ

So Paul's doctrine of the grounds for justification doesn't stop with step one. It's true that we are justified by grace, freely, without a cause. But while grace costs us nothing, it cost Jesus everything. Notice Romans 3:24 once more:

> Being justified freely *by His grace*
> through the redemption which is *in Christ Jesus*.

Grace is freely bestowed, but in another sense, it isn't free. We are justified freely by His grace *through* the redemption that came *in Christ Jesus.* In other words, we are justified not only by grace, we are also justified in Christ through the redemption which He accomplished on the cross. Romans tells us that God presented Jesus as a sacrifice of atonement through faith in His blood. We are justified not only by grace; we are also justified by blood.

Grace tells us that salvation is without a cause in me. That there is no cause in me that God would shower His love upon me. But blood tells me that salvation is not cheap; it cost Jesus everything! Grace, according to John 1:17, came by Jesus Christ. The indulgent parent illustration is not enough. If you preach only grace and never blood, then grace will result in presumption and permissiveness. We must understand that grace comes at the cost of the infinite life of the Son of God.

According to the Bible, the law and its consequences still stand; the wages of sin is still death (see Romans 6:23). Human action has led us to the place that we cannot fix ourselves. We cannot make ourselves right with God. Once that law is broken, once a person has made just a single "out," the law can never be kept perfectly. From that time on, obedience—doing right—can never become the basis for one's acceptance with God. Although such a rapid judgment may seem harsh and unbending, the reality is that once we start down the road of disobedience, it rarely ends with just one offense. One sin leads to another until we lose the ability to discern between right and wrong.

So there is no human way out for the sinner. You have to bat 1.000 to be saved, according to the law. And even if a human being, or an angel, succeeded in perfectly living out the laws of the universe, that obedience could save only that individual. It would be in response to his own achievement.

But I have good news. There is One whose nature transcends the limitations of humanity. He is the very One who made the law. The story of the Cross is the story of a God who came down to earth and assumed the limitations of human nature. Both God and the human race are perfectly represented in this divine-human Person. The whole human race participated in the perfect obedience of the man, Jesus. To all those who "fall short of the glory of God," Jesus offers the gift of His own perfect righteousness, earned in thirty-three years of perfect obedience here on earth.

But that raises an interesting question. How could the actions of one single man be counted equal to the actions of so many billions of people? How could one die in the place of so many? How could one man's acts of righteousness atone for so many people's sinful and imperfect acts? What kind of celestial compounding is taking place in the divine equation of salvation?

Let me ask a question that may seem unrelated for the moment: Which is greater, an artist or his artwork? The answer should be obvious. Long before a piece of art ever existed in stone or on canvas, it was conceived in an artist's mind. If something should happen to the art, the original artist would be capable of reproducing it. The artist is greater than the art.

Visiting St. Peter's Cathedral in Rome some time ago, I saw Michelangelo's beautiful statue, the *Pieta,* near the back of the nave on the right side. The marble sculpture shows a seated Mary holding in her lap the broken body of Jesus, taken down from the cross. The artistry is beyond magnificence; the very stone seems alive with motion. It is an authentic description of how the artist imagined the original scene.

One day a madman hid a hammer under his jacket and entered the cathedral. He approached the statue, whipped out his hammer, and began smashing it—blow after blow. First, one of Mary's arms fell to the ground, then her nose was shattered. Shocked onlookers finally restrained the man before he could do further damage. The greatest sculptors of Italy were called together to restore the priceless piece. Some eight weeks they worked diligently, desperately trying to restore the *Pieta* to its original beauty. Finally, the leader of the artists broke down in tears and said, "If only Michelangelo himself were here, he would know what to do."

Who is greater, the creation or its Creator? Once again the answer is obvious. Jesus is clearly greater than the creation. Not only did He make the moral law of the universe, He also made the entire universe. This explains why it could not be sufficient for an angel to die for us. It had to be the Creator. How much value, then, does Christ have? He is worth the entire universe because He is the One who made it all! When Jesus died on the cross, a value equal to the entire universe was in play. Because Jesus is the Creator, His death on the cross atones for every sin that ever was committed or ever could be committed. He is equal in value to all there is.

Some time ago I spent a month traveling throughout Europe to a number of ministers' meetings. On the way home, my baggage was lost, so I arrived without my socks and underwear! A day later, my family and I set out for a lengthy tour of the American West. Before we left, I bought a new set of socks and underwear. While crossing the North American continent, I kept phoning the airline to find out where my baggage was. "Probably in Copenhagen," the agent said, and that wasn't encouraging. Why am I telling you this? Because this whole experience thoroughly impressed me with the immensity of this great planet. Europe is vast enough by itself, but when I got back to the United States, I discovered another great continent.

I was impressed with the enormity of the task of creation. The circumference of the earth's surface is 24,000 miles. It would take at least a month to drive all the way around the earth at the equator—if one could! So vast is the world, and yet Jesus Christ made it all. But this planet is only a mere speck in the vastness of the universe. Our nearest neighbor in space, the moon, is about 240,000 miles away. It takes light about a second and a half to pass from the earth to the moon.

Compare that with the vastness of the universe. It takes light more than *ten billion years* to come to us from the further reaches of what we have so far discovered about our universe. And Jesus made the entire universe—every galaxy, every planet (see John 1:3). He is equal in value to every bit of it, and yet He chose to come down to this earth and to obey God perfectly for us. He came down and received the full consequence of our sin—eternal death, permanent extinction. At the Cross, the sins of the entire universe were rolled onto Christ.

At the Cross we discover infinite suffering, infinite humiliation, and infinite rejection. No one will ever be able to know what it meant for the Creator to be nailed to a cross, reserved for criminals, by His very own created beings! But by enduring the ultimate agony, He was atoning for the sins and shortcomings of His entire universe. Somehow, "in Christ" God has the legal right to count every sinner righteous before Him. This can be explained in different ways. People talk about substitutionary atonement, representative atonement, demonstrative atonement, and other ways of describing this transaction. But this much is perfectly clear: What God did in Christ is sufficient to place me in an entirely new relationship to Him. Because of the Cross, God has every right to count me righteous before Him. My old record is gone. A new and perfect record has taken its place. My best current efforts are acceptable to Him. And what Christ did is sufficient in value to redeem not just me, but the entire universe.

In human terms it may be impossible to explain adequately exactly how and why the great exchange between Christ and us takes place. But, for me, the following story helps a little bit. Although I have not been able to verify every detail, I share it as a path to understanding.

During the American Civil War, the early Adventist believers ran into a problem when they came to the conviction that military combat was inappropriate to Christian experience. Somehow Adventist young people needed to find a way in which they could serve this country without being involved in combat. Fortunately, the United States government had a special plan for young people in that situation. If a man could find a substitute who would be willing to go to war in his place, he wouldn't have to go himself. A young Adventist was called to serve in the army of the North. He happened to have a friend who was eager to help put an end to the rebellion! So the Adventist youth allowed his friend to join the Union army in his place. A short time later, his friend was killed at the battle of Shiloh.

About a year later, a letter came from the draft board informing the young Adventist that he had been drafted once again. He sent a reply advising the authorities that he could not be drafted because he was dead! The authorities had never gotten a letter like that before; the dead usually don't write! So they took the young man to court. The amazing thing is that he won the case! The court ruled that when his personal substitute died at Shiloh, this young person himself died to the draft. Legally, it was as if he himself were at the battle and lost his own life. As inadequate as this analogy may be, it helps me understand how the death of one could be accepted in place of another. Somehow, "in Christ" God has found the way to count all of us righteous before Him.

Paul talks about the great gospel transaction in these terms:

> He was made sin for us,
> even though he did not know sin,
> in order that we might become the righteousness of God
> in him (2 Corinthians 5:21).

This text tells me that, in Christ, God is fully able to count us righteous before Him. In some mysterious way, what God did on the cross produced a great exchange for the human race. Although the text doesn't explain the process as clearly as we might like, this much is clear: We don't have to remain in the condition of "having sinned and falling short." We *can* be right with God now. We *can* rejoice in who we are as a result of what Christ has done. To repeat Paul's language again, we are justified not only by grace, we are also justified in Christ.

If Paul had stopped here, he would have left the impression that *everyone* will be saved. Why? Because we are saved by grace, and God showers His grace upon all. We're also saved by the blood of Christ, and He died for all. His death had a value equal to the entire universe. This leaves no one out. It includes everyone who ever lived. In Christ, everyone has been atoned for on the cross. Does this mean that everyone will be saved whether or not they want to be? Not at all, as we shall see.

Through faith

Although everyone has been atoned for, not everyone will reap the benefits of that atonement. Actually, for several reasons, it would be a bad idea for everyone to be "saved."

49

1. If all sinners were accepted by God, without any change in attitude or character, it would introduce sin, chaos, and fear to the entire universe throughout eternity. A universe that goes on forever in the kind of chaos we live with today, is not very attractive. The day must come when sin is brought to an end.

2. Saving unreconstructed sinners would be bad for the sinners, too. Can you imagine unreformed alcoholics being forced to live forever in a place without bars or package stores? Compulsive gamblers forced to live without casinos and lotteries? That might be worse than hell for them, and God has no intention of turning heaven into hell.

3. Saving everyone would also be a bad idea because God respects human freedom. If some people don't want a relationship with God, He will not force it on them. God will not save everyone, because He respects a person's freedom to choose whether or not he wishes to be saved.

And so in Romans 3, Paul has one more thing to say about the way people come into a justified relationship with God. Justification occurs by grace and in Christ. But there is a third aspect to this issue of justification, and we find it in verse 25:

> Being justified freely *by His grace*
> through the redemption which is *in Christ Jesus*:
> whom God appointed ahead of time as an atoning sacrifice
> *through faith* in his blood.

Not only are we justified by grace and in Christ, but according to Paul, we are also justified through "faith." Whatever Paul means here by "faith," he does not mean that faith is the ground of our salvation. Faith cannot earn our justification, not in any way. We are justified because of something that happened in the heart of God (grace) and because of something that was done in Christ on the cross. Salvation never comes to a person because that person deserves it. Salvation is by grace and in Christ. Yet Paul says that we are also justified through faith. So the three pre-requisites by which people are justified are by grace, in Christ, and through faith.

FAITH!

To be justified by faith means that even though grace and Christ's blood provide all the ground we need to get right with God, justification is still something that we have to consciously desire and choose. Faith is not a work; it is a gift. And yet, faith is something that we exercise in the same way that we put our hand out to receive a gift. If we put our hand behind our back, we don't receive the gift. Faith is a gift, but it has to be exercised. It is a capacity that God grants us, yet it is also a choice that we must put into practice.

What, then, is faith, and how do I know when I have it? Saving faith is not a work, yet it never comes without works. Works are the evidence that our faith is genuine. When we have faith in Christ—faith in a justifying God—something happens to us. We're saved by faith alone, apart from works of law, but saving faith is never alone. Faith is more than just a mere mental assent to the gift of salvation. It is a daring trust in God. Faith means staking your life on God, saying "God, I'm going to accept Your salvation, no matter where it leads me and no matter what the cost." Salvation is free, but it leaves us changed people.

Jesus.

The best illustration I have ever seen of faith is the story of Blondin, a French tight-rope walker, who strung up a cable across Niagara Falls. In front of an audience, he walked across the chasm on the cable and returned. Everybody cheered. Then he said, "How many of you think I could walk across the falls pushing a wheelbarrow?" He did that successfully too, and everybody cheered again. Now he asked, "How many of you think I could make it across and back with a man in the wheelbarrow?" Just about everyone raised their hands, because his skill was obvious. But then he asked who would be the first to climb into the wheelbarrow—and all the hands came down!

Do you see the difference? One type of faith says, "Yes, I believe you can do it." The other type of faith stakes its life on that belief. Saving faith means that we stake our life on what God has done for us in Christ. When saving faith becomes a part of our lives, then everything we do, say, or live for is related to Christ. True faith is more than just a casual decision; true faith takes hold of us—body, soul, and spirit. True faith becomes the central focus of our lives.

That's the reason many people don't want salvation even though it is free. They don't want to give their lives over to someone else. They want to stay at the center of their personal universe. But for everyone who is willing to exchange the life he has for something better, the news is good. Jesus never fails to respond to that kind of willingness. If you tell Jesus that you want Him to be at the center of your universe, He will come without condition. You didn't bat 1.000? He did. When your best efforts fall short of the glory of God, you can still rejoice because you know that His best efforts are more than good enough.

But being saved by faith does not mean that it no longer matters what we do. Faith is never separated from the whole person. Those who are saved by faith become changed people. The decisions they make from that day forward are different decisions. Faith means you get into that wheelbarrow, and you go with Him—wherever He leads.

The practice of faith

In the real world, in practical terms, how do we respond to what Christ has done for us? How do I actually go about starting a relationship with God? What does it mean to respond to God's mighty act of salvation at the cross? What does it mean, in practice, to be justified by grace, in Christ, and through faith? I would like to suggest a few practical steps:

1. Acknowledge your need. We need to realize and freely admit that we haven't batted 1.000 or even come close. Unless we understand that and admit that, we can never come to Christ. That is the difference between a Pharisee and a publican. Pharisees have confidence in the quality of their "batting" efforts; publicans know that they are stuck in the minor leagues. They know that they need Christ if they are ever going to make it in this life or the next.

How can we become more aware of our need for God? Reading the Bible makes us aware of the kinds of things that tripped up the saints back then. The Bible portrays the deeds of its characters honestly—the good, the bad, and the ugly. Reading about David and Moses and Peter helps us become more aware of our own shortcomings. It is also helpful to pray that God will open up your self-understanding. Some have found it helpful to develop a spiritual diary in which they record the things that they learn about themselves from God and from the experiences of life. Consult also with trusted friends (more on these strategies in the last chapter of this book).The path to salvation begins with an awareness of our own need.

2. Desire and accept what Christ has done. Drink in the incredible value that has been assigned to you at the Cross.And you can have all that value today.You don't have to wait until you have "earned" it.As you read this, if you realize that you are not in Christ, that you are batting .240, that there is no chance you will ever make it by your own efforts, you don't need to remain out of touch with Christ's grace and blood a moment longer.You can choose to accept what He has done for you right now.

Do you really want to be right with God? Are you afraid of what you might lose? You are not alone. Nearly everyone is somewhat divided inside over the question of salvation. Part of you knows that you are in a mess, and you want desperately to get out of it.The rest of you clings to the mess and ticks off all the advantages of being in a mess! Take hold of that part of you that wants to be right with God, the part that wants to do God's will. Pray that God will give you a love for Him, a love for salvation, a love for the truth, no matter what the cost (more on this later in the book). I have found that when people pray that way, God provides.Accepting salvation involves cost, but the joy and freedom that come from being right with God are worth whatever one might have to give up.

3. Rejoice in what God has done for you. There's no reason to walk around with a long face when you realize that you are saved by grace in Christ. No matter where you've been or what you've done, God has done more than enough to save you.That is worth celebrating for the rest of your life!

But how do we maintain such an attitude of gratitude in a very cynical world? By *developing* an attitude of gratitude.There are thousands of good things in our lives that we have never thanked God for. When we learn to focus our attention on these things more than on all the frustrations of life, we will have much more joy and much more faith (more on this in the next chapter)!

4. Let every act of your life demonstrate your loyalty and trust in Him. Good deeds and faithful works are never the basis for your salvation, but they are the glorious result of that salvation. When you know that you are saved, and when you know that you can smile in Christ, it becomes so much easier to be all that you can be for Christ. It becomes a joy to serve and to bless others. It becomes a joy to share the faith that energizes you everywhere you go.

And forget about the batting average from here on. Let God count the batting averages. In Christ, our best efforts are acceptable to God. In Christ we are batting 1.000 today, tomorrow, and the next day— regardless of how we feel. And as we strive in Christ to make our lives more and more similar to the way He sees us, real changes will come. Our changing lives are a natural response to an incredible salvation that is free and available this very moment.

How is your life going right now? Are you finding yourself frustrated from day to day by your own shortcomings? The best way to know that you are living by batting averages, and not by grace, is how you respond to others. If your natural response to most of life's situations is to be critical, bitter, and constantly putting other people down, that is a sign that you're living by your batting average. If you know that you are batting .214, and you can find someone who is batting .188, it is natural to look at that person and say, "What's your problem?" A critical and faultfinding spirit is the clearest indication that we are living by our batting average and not by grace. The person who lives by grace knows two things: (1) he doesn't deserve it, and therefore he cannot point a finger at anyone else, and (2) in Christ, he has it anyway, so he no longer needs to build himself up by criticizing others.

Summary reflections on two chapters

Let me tie the biblical concepts in this chapter to the more behavioral categories of the previous one. All of us, as sinners in the biblical sense, are trying to secure a life independent of God. But life without God, without His cleansing and His acceptance, results in an insecure sense of self-worth. So to cover our insecurity, we construct a belief system that will give us worth. We attribute value to what we have, what we have achieved, and who we know. Possessions, performance, and people become the basis upon which we feel good about ourselves.

This is not only true of secular people; practicing Christians are vulnerable to this as well. We may even use our spiritual achievements as a measure of self-worth. When Christians are not sure whether God loves them and accepts them in Christ, they can be even more insecure than secular people because they know the high standards of performance taught in the Bible.

The problem is that whenever we turn away from God's grace and try to build ourselves up through our own efforts (whether secular or religious), we will always feel superior or inferior to others. We feel superior when things are going well or when we compare ourselves with the "losers" of our society. When we feel superior, we take comfort in the fact that we are not as "bad" as others are. But our confidence is misplaced and plunges us into a self-justifying illusion.

On the other hand, we feel inferior whenever we fail to live up to our own standards or whenever we come in contact with the "superstars" of achievement in our environment. While this inferiority is closer to reality than a phony superiority, it robs us of the confidence we need to make a positive difference in the world. When we live outside of God's acceptance, whether Christian or secular, we tend to swing back and forth between an illusory superiority and a depressing inferiority.

The gospel dispels this game. It creates a new self-image. The gospel humbles us in the presence of others because it teaches us that we are sinners saved only by grace. At the same time, it emboldens us before others when we realize that we are loved and honored by the only eyes in the universe that really count. The gospel gives us both boldness and humility. It gives us a boldness that needs no grounding in superiority. And it gives us a humility that doesn't depress. No mere philosophy or religion can accomplish this in us. We actually get free! We are no longer bound by lies.

Without the gospel, all our possessions, achievements, and relationships are tools to build or maintain our sense of worth. But when the gospel changes us, our possessions, achievements, and relationships stop being about ourselves because we don't need to derive our worth from them. We can use our possessions as we choose. We can focus our energies on achievements that really matter to us and to the world. And we can relate to others and enjoy them for who they are in themselves, not for how they make us feel about ourselves. It is a taste of real freedom, freedom that only comes with the gospel. Nothing else in the whole world comes close. We are freed to serve others, not to enhance our own status, but in gratitude for the ultimate service that was done for us on the cross.

The effect of the gospel is beautifully illustrated by a bedtime story told by Uncle Arthur (Arthur Maxwell was a favorite author when I was a kid). It is a story about the slave market in New Orleans early in the nineteenth century. A huge African man was up for sale. He was about six-foot-eight and weighed something like 280 pounds. He was powerfully built. If he were alive today we'd probably turn him into a football player. The auctioneer extolled the large amount of work that could be expected from such a man. There was only one problem. The whole time the auction was taking place, the man stood there in a defiant pose with his arms folded across his chest, saying, "I will not work! I Will Not Work! I WILL NOT WORK!"

The bidders in the slave market ignored his comments, and the bidding went higher and higher. One man in particular seemed especially interested in this African. He kept jumping in to raise the bid. Before long, the man was sold to him for the highest price ever obtained in the New Orleans slave market. As his new owner came up to claim him, the African spoke to him with some compassion, saying, "I know you paid a high price for me, but you need to know that I meant what I said. I will not work. You can shout at me, you can beat me, you can do whatever you want, but I will not work!"

"Let's not worry about that now," the slave owner said. "Just get in my wagon and I'll show you where you are going to live." After riding some distance out of town, the two men came to a lovely cottage surrounded by a white picket fence. The owner stopped the wagon and said, "This is where you will be living."

"This house is for me? Really? I didn't expect a place so nice!"

"Yes, this will be your home," the slave owner replied.

"That's very generous of you," said the slave. "You paid a high price for me, and now you give me this! But I still must tell you, I will not work. No matter what you do to buy my favor, I will not work!"

"That's OK," said the master. "You don't have to work for me. I bought you to set you free!" And with that, he signaled his horse, and the wagon began rolling away, leaving a startled African standing by the road in front of his new house.

"Stop! Stop!" The man ran after his former master. When the wagon halted, the former slave knelt down on the ground in front of the man who had purchased his freedom and said, "If you have truly set me free, I will serve you for the rest of my life!"

I detect just a hint in this story of the great transaction between Jesus and us that happens when we grasp the significance of the Cross for our lives. If Jesus has truly set us free at the Cross, is He not worth serving for the rest of our lives?

CHAPTER

3

KEEPING THE FAITH

The previous chapters address how, and on what grounds, people get right with God. They provide a basis for establishing a relationship with God. In this chapter we will look at the ongoing process of developing and maintaining a relationship with God. If we desire to lead secular people into a relationship with God, it is imperative that we ourselves have a relationship with Him. But we cannot take such a relationship for granted, even in Adventist churches.

One of the unforgettable moments of my life occurred when I was visiting with a pastor who worked outside North America. For a while I had great difficulty believing what he was telling me. He said that when the ministers got together privately, back home in his conference, the number one topic of discussion was whether God exists! I'm not talking about just any group of ministers, priests, or rabbis. These were Seventh-day Adventist ministers working in a Seventh-day Adventist conference in good and regular standing! I share this not to poke fun or vent my horror, but simply to point out that maintaining a living walk with God in the midst of a secular, technological age is no easy matter. The reality is that we have never faced a time in our history when Seventh-day Adventists have been more insecure about their faith in God or more insecure about being Seventh-day Adventists.

A time of spiritual crisis

Now, if you've been in the Church for forty or fifty years, you might not have experienced this insecurity as much as does my generation and the generation following mine. This insecurity afflicts those of us who grew up in the turmoil of the '60s—and their children. My generation is not necessarily more perverse or more lax in passing on the fundamentals than earlier generations. But for my generation, many things that have been handed down as certainties have proved to be questionable in fact. Some "truths" have seemed to be less about God's will and more about keeping certain people in power. Too many things that had made sense in the past turned out to be setups when viewed in the present. As a result, my generation felt betrayed and compelled to lay everything open to question. This has had positive as well as negative results. In this chapter, the focus is on the negatives—and some suggested remedies.

Of course, this experience of questioning earlier certainties, this sense of betrayal, is not limited to Seventh-day Adventists. The latter half of the twentieth century has been a time of convulsive change in every aspect of life. The advent of computer technology and the Internet has fundamentally changed the way people think and reason. The speed and complexity of life has accelerated rapidly. Nothing seems stable anymore. Jobs are downsized the minute your salary becomes comfortable. Families seem to have lost the key to stability and permanence. Where you live has become subject to chance more than intention. As a result, extended families have been ripped apart.

At a time when the foundations of everyday life seem to be collapsing with exponential speed, churches and other religious institutions have been shaken with devastating force by two great spiritual realities:

1. The general dominance of secular culture, first in the Western world and increasingly in the developing world as well. Secular thinking has undermined the institutions of religion at just the time when spiritual stability is most needed. The supernatural seems increasingly distant from reality. Conflicting interpretations of reality seem to discredit all claims to absolute truth. Expressions of faith have been shoved to the margins of consciousness as the five senses become the arbiters of truth.

2. New Age thinking. A second major reality has shaken the confidence of today's generations in Seventh-day Adventist faith. Toward the very end of the twentieth century, secularism was joined, and partially replaced, by an amorphous, feel-good spirituality known to many as New Age thinking. New Age spirituality spoke much about God and even affirmed the idea of prophetic "channels." At the same time it manifested little interest in the prophetic insights of the Bible or in the kinds of doctrinal concerns that had energized Seventh-day Adventist faith in the past. New Age thinking trivialized the moral basis for Seventh-day Adventist standards. In a real sense, New Age spirituality is the perfect complement of secular philosophy. Although spiritual in tone, it is no more friendly toward religious institutions or doctrinal convictions than secularism has been. So it is not surprising that Seventh-day Adventists have never been more insecure about what they believe or how that belief should be translated into everyday life and practice.

The process of secular drift

These large trends suggest to me that the report of discussions in a far-away conference regarding God's existence is probably not that far from where many of us live. If we do not consciously and intentionally cultivate a relationship with God, we will inevitably drift into secular or New Age modes of thinking. The drift into secular types of thinking doesn't happen overnight. People don't just wake up one morning and decide that they don't believe any more or that the teachings of their church don't matter. It usually happens gradually over a period of months or years. It is a process, a "secular drift." The process of secular drift involves several steps:

1. Personal, private prayer life is the first thing to go. The uncertainty plaguing faith in today's world often first shows itself in the area of private prayer. More than one pastor's wife has told me that her husband has not prayed in years, except in public. I do not imply an indictment of all Seventh-day Adventist pastors, but I believe that the struggle to maintain one's communication line with God is tougher now than it has ever been. How many of us have a prayer life that is all that it could or should be?

This particular issue is deeply personal. Not even your spouse may know that your personal prayer life is slipping. It takes place in that quiet time, all by yourself, when no one else is looking. This is the place where secular drift usually begins.

2. The study life begins to decline. I know of people who have not prayed for years, yet who continue a routine of study. They might not even go to church, yet they get up on Sabbath mornings and read the *Review, Our Firm Foundation,* or *Spectrum.* They may watch 3ABN on Saturdays instead of a football game or a movie. But without a strong prayer component, interest in spiritual subjects tends to decline over time, at least in terms of one's personal spirituality. When study continues in the absence of prayer, it may be less for one's own spiritual journey than to call in question the spiritual journeys of others.

3. Personal lifestyle standards begin to slip. A change in one's personal lifestyle is usually the first *public* indicator of secular drift. It's true that today many questions about the Adventist lifestyle have been raised and discussed. I cannot settle these issues here, but my years of experience as a pastor tell me that when a person relaxes his lifestyle standards in areas where before he had strong convictions, it is often a sign of secular drift.

I would encourage you to think seriously about the changes you make in your lifestyle. Many Adventists sincerely believe that wearing a wedding ring is not in harmony with God's will for them personally. Such a belief is not universally shared among Adventists, but it is part of a spiritual package that seeks to communicate modesty, simplicity, and God-given beauty. When a person begins to wear a wedding band, do they do so as a deeper way to glorify God? As a way to reaffirm a shaky marriage? Or as a socially-acceptable way to indulge a love of glitter? I have no question that many Adventists have chosen to wear wedding rings for reasons that strengthen their relationship with God. This paragraph is not directed at them. But my experience as a pastor has also taught me that when a change in lifestyle or standards is combined with a decline in the devotional life, it is almost always a sign of secular drift. The change in outward appearance is often the first public signal of a decline in the private spiritual life.

To focus merely on the issue of wedding rings or jewelry would be to miss the point. When lifelong abstainers start allowing beer or wine in their refrigerators, that is usually a sign of secular drift. When truthful people start bending the truth in the service of a good cause, that is usually a sign of secular drift. When honest people become comfortable cheating on their income tax, that is usually a sign of secular drift. When frugal people start showing more excitement over expensive toys than they do over helping the poor and oppressed, that is usually a sign of secular drift. When modest people begin startling you with their dress selections, that is usually a sign of secular drift.

I must not go on without a note of caution. As much as I believe in what I have written above, I realize that in a closed and dysfunctional church community, the observance of outward behavior can be used to do great harm. We drive people away from God when we arbitrarily impose our personal convictions on others who neither understand nor accept them. What I am calling for here is *a personal awareness of our own standing with God.* If we are aware of the markers of secular drift, we will be less likely to lose our personal connection with God. So the goal of this section is to encourage personal awareness; it is not a call for more Adventists to become "conformity police."

In an open, truly loving community, gentle lifestyle confrontation in an atmosphere of acceptance can sometimes help people make commitments to God that they would be unable to make alone. In my experience, however, such communities are rare among Adventists. In most situations it is healthier and more effective to apply the counsels of this chapter primarily to ourselves and not to others.

4. Inconsistent church attendance. The next step in secular drift is the effect it has on attendance at worship. Again, it is rare for a person to move from regular attendance to nonattendance in a short period of time. The fall off in church attendance may start with something as harmless as a "Winnebago Sabbath," taking the recreational vehicle and the family out into nature.

I can relate to the idea of spending Sabbaths away from public worship, because I have taken a few myself. If you are something of a public person within the Seventh-day Adventist Church, dropping in at a little, local church on Sabbath can be a draining experience. One day I showed up unannounced at a local church of twenty members. Before I knew it, I was teaching the Sabbath School lesson, preaching the sermon, and holding an "issues seminar" for three hours after the potluck. That evening I visited shut-ins, and the next day I made hospital calls! My family and I agreed that the next time we were on vacation and we were in the middle of nowhere, we should go off into the wilderness on Sabbath— anywhere but church. In my position, church and vacation don't always go together.

But you have to be careful with that type of thinking. Skipping church may start at a very innocent level, maybe one Sabbath here and another there. But then one Sabbath you just don't feel like getting up, and the next thing you know you are making it to church no more than once a month. One day you discover that it's a lot easier just to stay in bed or do something else. When one's attendance record reaches this stage, it is a major public signal that the walk with God is not what it used to be.

I realize that for Adventists who are deeply engaged in the real world, the church these days can become a very uncomfortable place. But while we should never tolerate spiritual or social abuse, I have a challenge for those who are uncomfortable with the "old ways." Don't be afraid to embrace the discomfort that the church can bring. Discomfort might be a word to you from God, a path toward personal growth. Discomfort and disturbance are among the ways that God cares for us, breaking through our tendency to become satisfied with wherever we are in our spiritual walk. If we run at the first sign of discomfort, we may be playing out a scenario of secular drift without out realizing it.

5. Doubts about the Bible and the afterlife. As secular drift progresses, doubts of all kinds begin to settle in with increasing frequency. You begin to question some of the things you have been taught. You become exercised over the "problem texts" of the Bible. You start challenging the pastor's sermons—in your mind at least—listening more with a critical ear than with a receptive heart. You pick up a Bible and try to read it, but a little voice in the back of your head says, "This is just ink on a page. This isn't some magical answer to all of life's problems. What are you wasting your time with this for?"

I realize that for some the Bible has been used as a tool of oppression or abuse. Ethnic groups have been told that they are inferior because the Bible says so. Women have been prevented from exercising some of their God-given gifts by well-meaning students of the Bible. Children have been required to "honor" their parents even when those parents were committing criminal acts. For such individuals, a certain amount of doubt may be an important step on the road to spiritual health. To grow spiritually, they may seem to be rejecting the Bible. But they are not really rejecting the Bible; they are rejecting false beliefs that have been wrongly based on the Bible.

More often, however, doubts come as the natural consequence of transgressing personal standards. Let me explain. When you act in a way that violates your conscience (or to put it in other terms, when you sin willfully), only two paths are open to you. You can repent of that sin or you can change your theology. The approach recommended in the Bible is to confess your sins, repent, and deal with the consequences. Going through this process leads to a sense of God's forgiveness and re-acceptance. It puts that sin behind you and restores your relationship with God.

But if you refuse to confess and repent, you will change in your relationship to truth. God has designed us to be uncomfortable when we violate our personal standards. So if we don't deal with our sins and our compromises, we will end up changing our view of right and wrong in order to avoid the pangs of conscience. Unconfessed moral violations force us to rationalize and justify our behavior to others and ourselves. Before we know it, our *beliefs* begin to conform to our *practice*. At the root of our deepest doubts about God, therefore, is a personal history of moral failure that has not been dealt with according to biblical teaching. And these kinds of doubts are a major signal of secular drift.

6. Growing distrust of religious institutions. The last step on the path of secular drift is a thorough distrust of all institutions, particularly religious institutions. It is a breakdown in one's loyalty to any kind of institution that stands for God. And this is a natural progression of the previous steps. Doubts about the Bible and the things you have been taught in the past progress to doubts about the pastor's ideas and the pronouncements of the conference. At its root is a rejection of spiritual authority in all its forms.

Rejection of religious authority within the Seventh-day Adventist Church used to be the unique domain of so-called "liberals." But this is no longer the case. These days, rejection of religious authority is as common in the so-called "right wing" of the Church as it is on the left. Is it possible that secular drift most affects those who are most certain that they are unaffected by it? Is it possible that this right-wing disrespect for our Church, its administrators, and its institutions may be rooted in secular drift? While no earthly institution, not even the Seventh-day Adventist Church, deserves unquestioning subservience, an attitude of disrespect, sarcasm, faultfinding, and criticism rarely goes hand in hand with a deep and vital relationship with God.

The antidote to secular drift

What can we do to counteract the devastating spiritual effects of secular drift? How can we maintain faith in a secular, New Age world?

The solution is not to take up a defensive posture and live in fear and suspicion. Instead we need to aggressively seize the reality of God's kingdom, which is alive and well in the midst of this secular, New Age world. The key is not to plot some kind of escape, but to proactively take hold of what God has already provided in Christ. According to the New Testament, the kingdom of God is already here, in the midst of this reality (see my book *What the Bible Says About*

The place to start

the End-Time, pages 75-83, for more on this New Testament perspective). Through the Holy Spirit we can have a walk with God that is real in a world that questions His very reality.

How do we do that in practice? The place to start is in the devotional life. As we suggested earlier, an emerging weakness in the personal, devotional life constitutes the first two steps on the road of secular drift. We need to slow down, to reflect, and become attentive to God's presence. The clearest message about God that most secular people will ever see is the one that they read in the life of some Christian they know. It would be a rare thing for us to lead a secular person into a living walk with God if we ourselves do not have one.

I grew up in New York City, one of the citadels of secularism. I've spent much of my adult life in higher education. Even serving as a church pastor for nine years did not shelter me from the corrosive effect of secular drift. Pastors often spend their lives running from one thing to another; from one idea to another; from one situation to another; from one emergency to another. And when you are dealing with spiritual things every day, a few secular thoughts may come to feel like a healthy break from the grind.

I have, therefore, put together a few ideas that have emerged out of the crucible of my own life. I offer them not as a cut-and-dried formula for everyone to follow. Instead, I offer them as a smorgasbord from which you can choose whatever seems appropriate to your circumstances. I have learned that, for me, four major things are necessary to prevent secular drift and to assure a vital relationship with God in a secular world—study, prayer, action, and witness.

Relationships are built on mutual communication. This involves both listening and talking. We learn about the other person through listening, and we share our inner selves through speaking about the things that matter to us. But a difficulty arises when it comes to our relationship with God. How do you talk to someone you can't hear, see, or touch? How do you listen to someone you can't hear, see, or touch? The part about talking to God is not so strange. We can do that in prayer. But how do we listen to a God whose voice we cannot hear?

The study life

The place where we can most clearly hear God's voice today is in His written Word. So a foundational step toward a living relationship with God begins with serious time in the study of God's Word and in other writings of high spiritual value, such as those of Ellen White. But not everything in the Bible is of devotional benefit. The selections we make for study, therefore, may be as important as the amount of time we invest in that study. In the suggestions that follow, I want to help you avoid some of the mistakes I have made in seeking a closer walk with God.

1. What we study must be relevant to everyday life. The choice we make of devotional materials should be sensitive to what is currently going on in our lives. If what you need at a particular point in time is recovery from alcohol abuse or from a painful past, "twelve-step literature" may be the best devotional reading for you at that time. On the other hand, if your deepest need is for a better understanding of the Bible, then devotional commentaries, such as the *Bible Amplifier Series*, may be just the ticket. The devotional life should address the basic issues that you are wrestling with. Otherwise it is not likely to affect your life. It will simply be an isolated pocket in the middle of nowhere.

2. Devotional study needs to focus on the person of Jesus. Since Jesus is the One through whom God has interacted most plainly with the human race, a focus on the person of Jesus is crucial for human beings who want to know God. In your choice of reading materials, highlight those that help you to understand Jesus better. In the Bible, the four Gospels and many of Paul's letters have a preferred place in devotional study. In the writings of Ellen White, books such as *The Desire of Ages* and *Steps to Christ* are designed for becoming better acquainted with God in the person of Jesus.

Some parts of the Bible and the Spirit of Prophecy may not be conducive to a growing devotional experience with God. For example, 1 Chronicles is inspired but it's not on the "recommend reading" list for the devotional life. The endless lists of genealogies and officers of David's court are useful to archaeologists and others interested in the names and historical sequences that are part of the context in which the Bible was written. But they are not well suited to our devotional needs. Likewise, a book such as Ellen White's *Counsels on Diets and Foods* may be extremely valuable for its purpose, but it does not always focus on the relationship with Jesus. A thorough knowledge of which foods are healthful or unhealthful may be of great importance, but it does not necessarily bring us closer to Jesus.

3. *Devotional reading cannot be rushed*. Devotional reading should be recreational. Try to arrange matters so that you don't have to set an alarm or limit the time you spend. Rushed devotionals can do more harm than good. I used to pick up the Bible, *The Great Controversy* or *The Desire of Ages* and challenge myself to read as many pages as I could in an hour. Before long it became a contest. I was motivated by secular goals more than by my desire to know Jesus better.

When it comes to devotional reading, take your time. It would be better to spend a whole hour on one text, and thoroughly explore what that text has to say, than to read page after page but experience minimal impact on your life. The pace of life has been accelerating for more than a generation now. In our technological age, we desperately need to learn how to slow down, to reflect, and to take stock of our lives. We need to let our racing hearts cruise down to idle for a while and just commune with God. If we don't take time to reflect, we may find ourselves further and further from a personal relationship with God—even in the midst of direct service for Him.

4. *Develop a devotional journal*. One of the most important insights of my life has been the adage, "Paper remembers; people forget." When I was younger and my mind was less cluttered than it is now, it seemed I could remember everything that mattered. But things have changed. Information flies by in such huge quantities that important things are continually falling through the cracks if I don't write them down. I find that some of my most important spiritual insights flash by and then fade into forgetfulness. In today's world, I can't afford to let God be crowded out, even by a multitude of good things.

Not only does paper remember the things I forget, the act of writing also seems to implant things more deeply in my mind. "Expression deepens impression." I say things in my mind as I prepare to write. I see the words I am writing. I feel the pen and the pressure on the paper. I am bringing a variety of learning modes into play. This helps what I write become a more permanent part of who I am as a person. Not only that, the process of writing seems to draw out thoughts and feelings that had been hidden from me before.

I believe, therefore, that one of the best ways to develop a closer walk with God is to journal, to write down the insights you gain from reading the Bible or other spiritual books. Don't write down just any spiritual insight. For your devotional journal, write down only those insights that make a deep impact on your soul. If you write down everything, the journal may become too cluttered to be helpful. The best devotional book you will ever read is the one you write for yourself. No two human beings are alike. A power-packed collection of insights that have moved you in the past will be a powerful resource to maintain and restore your relationship with God in the future.

One day I spent forty-five minutes reading a spiritual book. It filled my heart so much that I had to make notes on the experience. Not finding paper and pen to write with, I reached for my notebook computer and sat down. For more than an hour, I found myself keying in the insights the Lord gave me that morning. Most of those would be forever forgotten if I hadn't done that. Whether you journal important spiritual insights using paper and pen or the computer, the emerging "book of insight," your very own book of devotional reflections, will be a powerful tool that God can use to become more real in your life.

5. Develop a reflective diary. Through a "book of insight," in which you record the special concepts that encourage you in your relationship with God, you enhance your ability to "listen" to God's Word. But there is another way that journaling can enhance your ability to listen—the reflective diary. I call it my "book of experience."

It seems that most of the spiritual giants throughout history kept spiritual diaries. Ellen G. White did, and so did Luther, Wesley, and many others. What do we find when we read those spiritual diaries? There people reveal their inner struggles. They unveil a sense that God communicated with them directly in one way or another. They chart their progress through life's challenges.

I like to get a blank journal page in front of me and ask the Lord such questions as, "How do You feel about the way I treated my son yesterday? My wife? What are some ways that I can improve the class I'm teaching? How can I find a way to reconcile these two colleagues who are estranged?" Then I begin to write, letting the writing take me wherever it will. Often I find myself in places I hadn't planned to go, but to which God was clearly leading me. Sometimes I come to the realization that I talk too much in small groups or fail to express caring to my students or expect too much from my children. I may have been ignoring someone who really needed me. Sometimes I just total up my reflections on the last day or the last week; it's sort of like keeping score. I can detect trends in the course of my walk with God that I would miss if I did not take the time to reflect in this way.

The Lord uses that reflective time to teach me the value of listening to Him. When I go back and read these reflections later, they continue to be relevant. I've learned that if I don't keep score of my life and my behaviors, I tend to make the same errors over and over again. So keeping a reflective diary, or a book of experience, can play an extremely important role in our relationship with Jesus.

A life of prayer

When it comes to a relationship with God, talking to Him in prayer seems much more straightforward than listening to someone we can't hear. Nevertheless, a personal prayer life is the greatest challenge that most Christians face in life. Time and again Christians set out to improve their prayer life only to feel as if they have been shot down in flames. I have had the experience of failure in prayer many times. But over the years I have learned a number of things that have greatly helped me. I share them here in the hope that your next attempt to upgrade your own prayer life will be more successful than perhaps you have been before.

1. Any which way you can. There is no single right way to pray. Some people will tell you that the only appropriate bodily position for prayer is on your knees with eyes closed and hands folded. And, to be honest, that's the way I do it myself more often than not. But the Bible does not portray any kind of exclusiveness regarding the bodily position for prayer. People described in the Bible prayed standing up, on their knees, and flat on their faces. They prayed with eyes open and with eyes shut. They prayed with hands folded or with hands outstretched in the air. More important than a particular bodily posture is to connect with God.

Being aware of this has important consequences. For example, whenever I pray silently with my eyes closed, my mind tends to wander. I close my eyes to pray, and fifteen minutes later I find myself wandering in some other county. I usually have no idea how I got there. I was just in some kind of mental drift. Therefore, I find it most helpful to keep my eyes open when praying and to focus them on some object in the room, such as the pattern in a carpet or a couch. To focus my eyes helps me to focus my mind as well. I wonder how many people struggle in prayer simply because they don't know that God doesn't mind if we keep our eyes open when we pray. What matters is that our minds are focused on Him.

2. Finding a focus through the journaling process. I've found that another way to focus my mind is through the writing process. But this time, instead of recording insights about the Bible or about my own experience, I direct the writing to God Himself. Have you ever written a prayer to God? It's like writing a letter to Him. It can be a wonderful experience. I find that when I take the time to carefully shape the wording of a prayer or letter to God, the prayer becomes much more meaningful. The whole process of writing helps to draw out of me what I really want to say to God—things I might not have brought to consciousness any other way.

A "book of prayer" is the place where your God-directed thoughts gain focus and are recorded to be read again another day. If you are into computers, you might want to think of the prayer process as something like email. The "book of experience" records what you think God wants to say to you about your relationship. The "book of prayer" records what you want to say to God. As our experience with email teaches us, writing is a marvelous way to develop relationships even though we may not be physically with the person to whom we are writing. And social scientists have noticed an interesting feature of email. People somehow feel safer in email than they do in any other type of communication. They are willing to say things that they would never put in a formal letter or say to someone's face. So this can be an effective way to be more authentic with God in prayer.

If the concept of a "book of prayer" seems a bit unorthodox to you, just remember that the vast majority of the psalms are written prayers. What was good for the saints of old can still play a role in our relationship with God today! This is an aspect of "old-time religion" that many traditionalists have forgotten.

3. *Let prayer go to the core.* It is easy in prayer to pay a hurried visit to the missionaries and the colporteurs and fail to dig deeply into the depths of who you are and how your relationship with God is going that day. One reason that prayer may seem irrelevant to everyday life is that the crucial elements of everyday life are not brought to God while in the attitude of prayer. Discuss with God the very things that your journal has revealed are of utmost concern to you at a given time. Share with Him the events of the previous day. Share with Him your concerns about the implications of those events.

Prayer becomes truly meaningful when we are willing to open ourselves to God, to discuss the things that matter most to us, to share our deepest thoughts with Him. If prayer is not the place when you can share the things you wouldn't tell even your spouse, whom are you going to tell? Personal prayer may be our best chance to share with Somebody who knows and cares and accepts us just the way we are. We can safely talk to God about the things that we wouldn't dare tell another human being, not even a counselor sworn to secrecy. After all, nothing we could say will shock or surprise God.

He already knows, and He loves us just the same. It is safe to open even our darkest depths to Him.

4.Allow God to answer your prayers. Another helpful strategy is giving God the opportunity to answer your prayers. It is easy to rush through a prayer list and then bounce to our feet and move on with the day, never expecting that God might respond in some way. We say, "Lord, I am in a hurry today. Got to get ready for work, but there are missionaries and colporteurs out there that need some help. Well, got to run now, goodbye."

I encourage you to try something different the next time you are in the attitude of prayer. Have some paper and a pen in front of you, and when you are done with your prayer, take up the pen and wait. Write down whatever comes to your mind. Some of it may be silly or irrelevant. That has certainly been the case with me. But on some days, God just about scheduled my whole life! In the quietness of that moment He has brought to mind people that I need to visit or call.

I shared this idea in class one day at the Seminary. A student from Canada was moved to try it that night. After prayer he had the repeated feeling that a certain woman in Canada needed to be contacted. Since his wife was in Canada at the time, not far from where the woman lived, he decided to call his wife and ask her to contact the woman for him. The next day his wife called back and said that she had been unable to get through. He urged his wife to keep trying. He felt strongly that the Lord had some reason why this woman needed to be called at that time. The wife called once more. This time the woman answered. Her response was stunning. "A week ago my husband died, and I just got home from the doctor who told me that I have cancer. I've been sitting here by the phone wondering if anybody cared." My Canadian student now has no doubt that God can still communicate with His people today!

5.An emphasis on thankfulness. Glenn Coon, one of my all-time favorite preachers, used to emphasize Nehemiah 8:10: "The joy of the Lord is your strength." Coon believed that the secret of spiritual power is the joy that comes from a spirit of thankfulness and praise.

It is impossible to be sad for long when you are continually reciting the ways in which God has blessed and enriched your life. My experience over the years has clearly confirmed Coon's insight.

While Coon's strategy sounds simplistic and corny, it really works. He suggested spending a little time each morning writing down ten things for which you are thankful. During the course of the day, each of these items can become the focal point of a brief prayer. "Thank You Lord for the air." "Thank You Lord for the cat (or dog)." "Thank You Lord for the red roses." Very down-to-earth, practical stuff. This kind of prayer gets right down to the very basics of life. It brings us a sense of God's concern for every detail of life. And the amazing thing is, that as we thank the Lord for specific actions that have affected our lives, an incredible sense of confidence and joy takes over. You can't think of anything that you're thankful for? Get out a dictionary. "Apes," "apples," "apricots"—you'll find plenty of things on every page that you have never thanked God for! And the process is well worth the effort. Nothing can brighten our lives like a spirit of thankfulness and praise.

Digression: finding time

How can we find time for study and prayer in the midst of the crushing load of responsibility most of us bear? After all, few people have the time to accomplish all that they expect to accomplish in a day. That means that it is ultimately up to us to decide what is truly worth our time and what is not. When new activities clamor for involvement, it is crucial to realize that you can't add anything to your life without taking something else away.

The problem is that most people prefer not to make such choices. They seek to accomplish everything that is set before them, and it just does not work. Inevitably, either the family or the devotional life—or both—are sacrificed on the altar of indecision. So these days, whenever someone asks me to accept a position or perform a task, I ask myself the question""What activity will this replace? Is this more important or interesting than what I will have to give up in order to do this?" Life is a choice. If we don't choose, time will choose for us. And we will be unhappy with the choice.

All this has large implications for the devotional part of life. Our time with God is often crowded out by the press of lesser concerns. If we don't choose to spend the best part of every day with God, we will inevitably drift in a secular direction. So the first step in enhancing our devotional experience is to choose to make it a front-page priority in our lives. The great thing about will power is that it is strengthened by use. Choose to put God first. Say it out loud. Write about it to your friends. Expressing that choice will make the choice stronger. Decide what in your life needs to go if your devotional experience is to grow. Be careful about adding new assignments or responsibilities. In the devotional life, above all other things, we must echo the words of Paul, "This one thing I do, setting all other things aside" (see Philippians 3:13).

Lifestyle matters

If you want to maintain faith in a secular world, you've got to have more than just an interior life. Prayer and study alone are not enough. Without concrete and practical faith-action in the life, the devotional experience can easily become confined to a closet in one's mind. This leads to a schizophrenic existence in which faith affects the life for only a short time each day, followed by an essentially secular existence the rest of the time. Doing battle with secular drift calls for more than just the devotional experience, as effective as that may be.

In his book, *The Human Puzzle*, David G. Meyers confirms what Ellen White taught a hundred years ago—what a person believes may have relatively little impact on how he lives. What happens in the devotional life will have little impact on everyday experience unless accompanied by conscious, corresponding action. When people survey conservative Christian churches, including Adventist churches, they discover that the typical conservative Christian church may have virtually as much adultery, physical and sexual abuse, alcohol problems, and drug use as the nonchurched culture; the problems are just less visible in the church setting. This is particularly true of the Adventist setting, because our high behavioral standards make it socially unacceptable to confess sins such as adultery, alco-

What we do will ultimately shape what we think - thoughts conform to actions. (This statement does not reflect the ground of our faith but the result)

hol use, drug use, and the abuse of children or spouse. Our high standards can create an environment in which help and healing rarely occur. Quite often, therefore, belief in Adventist teaching has relatively little impact on how people live.

The other way around, fortunately, is very different. How you live has a powerful impact on what you believe. This is a major theme of the chapter in *The Ministry of Healing* called "Mind Cure" (pp. 241-259). The routine actions of daily life have a massive effect on what people believe and how they feel and think.

That is one of the secrets of the Seventh-day Adventist lifestyle. It compels us to bring God into every detail of our existence. When you're making out your family budget, what is the first thing you consider? The tithe. God is at the center of your financial life. When you are shopping at the clothing store, what are you thinking about? "If I were to wear this, would it enhance my Christian witness or would it distract from it or contradict it? Would this clothing glorify me or point to what God is doing in my life?" When you are in the grocery store, you are reading labels. Why? Because you don't want to take into your body things that God wouldn't approve. Things that might hinder your effectiveness for Him. Rightly handled, the Seventh-day Adventist lifestyle brings God into all the activities of daily life.

The strongest safeguard against secular drift—and even a secular psychologist will tell you this if you ask—is a seven-day-a-week religion. It is a faith that in some way affects every moment of every day of our lives. I was somewhat amused to discover that on many of the Caribbean islands, Adventists are known as "Seven Days." When I arrived for a camp meeting in the Bahamas, the newspaper declared, "Speaker Arrives for Seven Days Conference." I wish that were not just a misunderstanding, but a statement of our worldwide reality! Adventism cannot afford to be isolated in the closet of our experience. To be effective in a secular world, Adventism must affect the whole of our experience in this world.

This whole-hearted style of life is no denial of justification by faith—it simply recognizes that when Christ offers the gift, He also makes a claim. We practice God's lifestyle because we *have been*

Textual evidence?

accepted by God, not in order to earn His acceptance. Though the apostles were clear that salvation was a gift, the great rallying cry of the first-century Christian church was, "Jesus is Lord." To modernize that terminology a bit results in something like, "Jesus is the Boss." When first-century Christians said, "Jesus is Lord," they mean, "He has the right to tell me what to do and how to live."

The relationship between justification and lordship is most effectively illustrated by a story Jesus told His disciples. In Matthew 18:23-35 a king forgives his servant a debt of 10,000 talents (perhaps $10 billion in inflated currency). It is assumed in the story that the servant would gladly respond by forgiving his fellow servant a debt of a mere one hundred days' wages. There is shock all around when he does not. The story is a parable of divine and human forgiveness. What God does for us becomes a model for how we should treat one another. A balanced, living faith includes both devotion and action. We are saved by faith alone, but saving faith is never alone!

So, while devotions are vital to a living relationship with God, they will fail in their purpose unless our walk with God permeates our experience in the real world. Through the Seventh-day Adventist lifestyle we have the opportunity to experience God at the center of every detail of our lives. Through our practice of the faith, our beliefs become stronger, and our whole experience is integrated into our walk with God.

Sharing our faith is not an option

Related to putting our faith into daily practice is the importance of sharing our faith with others. In order to keep our faith strong it is necessary to share it. This is true not only for today; it has always been a fact of spiritual life. In the Old Testament context, the key to bringing the power of God into the lives of His people was to recite over and over the things that God had done for them in their past history.

Consider the plight of King Jehoshaphat. According to 2 Chronicles 20, he was under attack by the armies of three nations! He called his council together, but instead of developing a military or diplomatic strategy, he led them in prayer. Now, how would you and I pray in that situation? Wouldn't we probably succumb to abject and pitiful pleading? Instead, Jehoshaphat said, "Lord, You brought us out of Egypt with a mighty hand and an outstretched arm; You brought us through the wilderness. And when we got to the Promised Land, as You promised us, there were hostile nations all around. You told us to leave them alone, and now they are coming against us. You took care of us then. You can do it again. Our eyes are upon You."

As Jehoshaphat was recounting the acts of God, the power of the Exodus experience was manifested again. Instead of a battle, the enemy armies were dealt with by the choir. They sang a song and blew them right out of town. The power of God that divided the Red Sea and fed His people in the wilderness returned to them in response to Jehoshaphat's retelling of the Exodus. Reciting what God has done for you in the past brings His power back into your life in the present.

Expression deepens impression. Talk faith, and you will have more faith. Ellen White expresses this idea forcefully:

It is a law of nature that our thoughts and feelings are encouraged and strengthened as we give them utterance. While words express thoughts, it is also true that thoughts follow words. If we would give more expression to our faith, rejoice more in the blessings that we know we have,—the great mercy and love of God,—we should have more faith and greater joy. No tongue can express, no finite mind can conceive, the blessing that results from appreciating the goodness and love of God" (*Ministry of Healing*, pp. 251-253).

Can you remember a time when you shared your personal testimony with a friend or even a stranger? You told of the helplessness of your human condition. You also shared the excitement and joy that came with the discovery that Christ died for you personally. Whenever the cross of Christ is uplifted, the Holy Spirit presses the claim of the Cross home with power to whomever is listening. And that same power spills back to the one who testifies. Can you remember how the act of sharing your faith confirmed your own faith?

I am rarely so confident and secure in my walk with God as I am when I share with others what He has done for me.

If these things are so, why do we witness so little? A major deterrent to sharing faith in a secular world is that we sense that witness often oversteps the boundaries of social propriety. When we think of witness, we often think of badgering people and intruding into their lives. The golden rule comes into effect here. "Do unto others as you would have them do unto you." I have spoken to hundreds of Adventists whose conscience bothers them concerning the way they attempt to share their faith. The end result is miserable. Many Adventists feel guilty when they witness, and they feel guilty if they don't. That is no way to live.

We can be freed to witness again when we find out that *true* witnessing has two basic principles that keep us from overstepping the boundaries of social propriety.

The first principle: Before you can get a person to listen to you, you have to put them at ease; they need to be comfortable. To rail at somebody on a street corner may cause the opposite of what you intend. Do you enjoy being with people who repeatedly tell you what to do and who put you down by highlighting their own superior understanding? Do they make you feel at ease? Do you feel like listening any further to what they have to say? Would you want to become like them?

Putting people at ease means avoiding the attitude of a superior. Putting people at ease means relating to them in such a way that they are comfortable in one's presence. It means investing more time in listening than in talking, at least at first. Jesus certainly had that ability, for prostitutes and sinners loved to be around Him. We have to "earn" the right to confront others about the central issues in their lives. We earn that right through genuine caring that is more willing to listen than to instruct. It is not necessary to put people down or to nag them in order to share one's faith.

The second principle of true witnessing is to live an attractive, Christ-centered style of life. Most secular people are looking for something better. When they see people who "have their act together," they find it incredibly attractive, far more attractive than the painted-on smiles of the media. People love to be with others who are at peace with themselves. They like people who listen to them and who don't put them down. A good test for the attractiveness of my Christian walk is: How do children—both mine and others—respond to me? Do children enjoy being around me? Or do they tend to shy away fearfully? If you put children at ease, you are probably putting their parents and other adults at ease by the same approach.

Sharing our faith in the secular world is a major challenge. We need to learn a whole new way of expressing our faith. We need to learn how to do so without crossing social barriers in ways that can end a relationship. The main point of this chapter, however, is that sharing our faith is important not only because secular people need Christ, but because we also need the spiritual strength and affirmation that come when we share our faith. Keeping the faith in today's world cannot be taken for granted. It is the result of a conscious effort to know God.

Lifestyle Matters: A taste of Heaven (Diet)
         "   "   2 Robes of Righteousness (Dress)
         "   "   3 Keeping the Faith - Sharing the (witnessing) Faith
#1   "   "   4 Seventh-Days Adventists
         lost people matter to God (Sabbath Remembering)
         "   "   5 Entertaining Angels (work Entertainment)
         "   "   6 Worship that Rocks!

Principles
#1 Jesus is Lord pg 78
#2 Faith without works will die
#3 We are all saved as individuals but called to live out our faith lives in community.

81

CHAPTER

4

IMPRESSIONS, IMPRESSIONS

For many Christians the greatest barrier to developing a living relationship with God is the lack of consistency in personal, private prayer. We touched on this issue in the previous chapter. In this chapter and the next we will examine some difficult issues in relation to prayer. The focus of this chapter is God's answers to prayer. A major disincentive to consistent prayer is the sense that it is only one-way communication. We talk to God, but He never answers back.

Or does He? How can we know God's answers to our prayers? Does God still speak with a living voice today or do we need to guess His will through the chain of circumstances that follow prayer? Would you know God's voice if you heard it? Could you pick His voice out from among the many voices that assault you in today's world?

Suppose you are a farmer. One day you are standing in your fields with your foot up on the front tire of your tractor. You look over the fields with satisfaction; it's good land; you've worked it hard over the years; it doesn't get much better than this. Suddenly you hear a voice behind you saying, "Plant corn instead of wheat this year." Would you do it? If you knew without a doubt that it was the voice of God, would you plant corn? But how would you know?

Suppose you are a single mother juggling a job and three children. It seems that you never have a moment's rest. Then one day you hear a voice behind you saying, "Invite your elderly parents to move in." Would you do it? If you knew without a doubt that it was the voice of God, would you do it? But how would you know for sure?

Suppose you are a lay person in a local church. God has blessed you through the years in your attempts to serve the church. You have been faithful in tithes and offerings. But then one day a voice behind you says, "Sell all that you have and give it to ADRA to feed the hungry." Would you do it? If you knew without a doubt that it was the voice of God, would you do it? But how would you know?

If God spoke to you today, would you know it was God?

I remember an elderly rancher. He'd been quite successful. In fact, he had one of the largest ranches in his country. In his old age, all of his hopes for the future were settled on his son. Early one morning he was awakened by a voice that said, "Take your only son up to that hilltop twenty miles north of you, stab him to death, and then set fire to him." If you had been that rancher, would you have done it? If you knew that God was the One telling you to do this, would you do it? How would you know?

How did Abraham know that this strange request had come directly from God? Frankly, it was a good thing that Abraham wasn't a Seventh-day Adventist because if he were, he probably wouldn't have gone to Mount Moriah. A committed Seventh-day Adventist would have compared what the voice said with the Scriptures and would have concluded, "This is not from God." You see, the voice was telling him to do something that was contrary to the sixth commandment. Not only that, the prophets reveal that to sacrifice one's son is an abomination unto the Lord. A good Adventist would be led to conclude that the voice was obviously not God's voice. There's only one problem. It *was* God's voice!

How did Abraham know that the voice telling him to do something contrary to God's will was from God? I suspect that in his long life Abraham had done a lot of walking and talking with God. He had come to know when God was communicating with him and when it was simply his own inner feelings or some other influence. Abraham had experimented with God. He had tested his impressions. He had practiced what he had heard. And he had figured out when it was God speaking and when it was not.

God is probably not going to ask you to do anything similar to what He asked Abraham to do. Only someone with a lifetime's experience of walking with God could possibly have responded the way Abraham did to God's request. God knew who He was dealing with. Abraham proved faithful to God, even in a tortured and perplexing situation. Through his example, God was able to teach the whole universe something special about His plan of salvation (see *Patriarchs and Prophets*, pp. 153-155). There is no telling what God can do with someone who is open to hearing and obeying His voice.

A living relationship with God

If we would like to have the kind of relationship with God that Abraham had, then we need to learn to recognize and know God's voice in our everyday lives. I suggest that there are only two kinds of Christian living. One kind could be described as "going through the motions." The other is based on a genuine, living experience with God.

"Going through the motions" is like having one's spiritual life on autopilot. You go to church on Sabbath morning. God is being worshiped, but your mind is on autopilot. You go through the hymns on autopilot. During the prayer, you're thinking about the afternoon. And how could anyone listen to a sermon while wrestling to keep the kids from disturbing everyone else? Forget it! Autopilot in the spiritual life can easily become a way of life.

Is your Christian life on autopilot? Do you do the Christian thing because your parents do it? Because your family does it? Because your best friends do it? Over the years as a pastor, I came to recognize that a high percentage of men, in particular, were in church mostly because their family attended. There was no strong personal commitment.

Do you go to church simply because it's a habit? Because you grew up going, and so you continue doing it? Does life get interesting for you only when you are at your job or on the golf course or at the mall—doing something of a secular nature? Is that where you feel the most alive and involved with life?

I would suggest that the only kind of Christian living that matters is the second kind—a genuine living experience with God. You know that God exists, and you know that He is with you, and you know that you can share your deepest needs and concerns with Him. And you know that He will do the same with you. A living, genuine relationship with God is the basis for the only kind of Christianity that really matters.

What to do with impressions

In the previous chapter we have seen that careful study, prayer, an integrated lifestyle, and the sharing of our faith are the best ways to counteract secular drift. But one further element of Christian experience is often left out of Adventist discussions of the subject. A crucial foundation to a living walk with God is understanding what to do with impressions. What do you do when you sense that God is trying to get through to you personally? How seriously can you take impressions to say and do and believe things, especially when the impression deals with an issue not addressed in Scripture?

I'm not talking about audible voices here. If you were to tell me that you hear audible voices all the time, I would listen to you, but I would be a little concerned. When I talk about impressions I have had, I am not making any special claim to God's favor. I don't hear audible voices, and I don't believe that my experience with God is unusual in any way. Yet I've come to know by experience that God is capable of communicating with me even though no audible voice is heard, even though no angelic figure is seen. The Bible suggests that God wants to communicate with us directly, so when we pay attention to God's voice outside of Scripture, we are being faithful to Scripture.

Being attentive to God's voice is vital to a living relationship with Him. Frankly, although the Bible and the Spirit of Prophecy are essential guides to Christian life, they don't specifically cover most situa-

Decisions Decisions

tions in life. No direct and specific message in inspiration covers most of the detailed decisions you face on an average day. For example, does the Bible tell you who would be the best person for you to marry? Does it tell you where you should live? Does it tell you what kind of job you should seek or what kind of education you should get? Biblical principles certainly apply to the decision-making process in such situations, but the actual choice is usually left up to us.

Daily Decisions not

Therefore, many of the most crucial, everyday decisions of life are not governed by a direct word from God in Scripture or the Spirit of Prophecy. Not everyone is willing to accept this. It is tempting to use a variety of interpretive approaches to the Bible and the Spirit of Prophecy in order to discover direct counsel for daily existence. The result is often to make both the Bible and the Spirit of Prophecy say things that the authors themselves would never have recognized. I do believe, however, that God would like to guide us in the most critical decisions of life. These decisions would be based on the principles of Scripture and the Spirit of Prophecy. But beyond these principles, God would like to offer us guidance in very specific and direct ways. He would also like to warn us of personal spiritual and physical dangers.

Take my experience at Lost Lake, for example, the location of one of the camp meeting programs for the Upper Columbia Conference. It was about thirty-five miles from the nearest small town and about fifteen miles from the nearest road on my map of the state of Washington. I was scheduled to speak at that camp meeting a few years ago.

I like the change of pace that traveling provides. I like seeing new places and meeting new people. So normally, when a trip is coming up, I am looking forward to it with a certain amount of anticipation. But that wasn't the case this time. Instead I had a general sense of unease, almost dread, and I just couldn't figure out why. Why was it that every fiber of my being was saying that I didn't want to go on this trip?

Once we were packed and started heading toward Lost Lake through Indiana, Illinois, Wisconsin, Minnesota, and South Dakota,

Warning

Danger

plus

the sense of general unease began to crystallize into a more specific sense of danger on the highway. I didn't say anything about my feelings to anyone else in the family; I just became a little more alert while driving and a little more careful than usual. I also didn't complain that my wife was content to let me do most of the driving!

Things passed fairly uneventfully until we reached western Montana and the interstate highway began to climb into the Bitterroot Mountains. My van is very reliable, but it has a little four-cylinder engine, which slowed us to about twenty-five miles per hour on the steep upward grade. At one point a truck came along behind me, moving just slightly faster than I was. He pulled out to pass. When he got alongside me, the road flattened out a bit, and my van surged forward. We seesawed back and forth for a minute or so, sometimes the truck was gaining on me, and then the van would regain some of the ground. Suddenly I saw yellow flashes of light to my left. I realized that the driver of the truck had lost track of my presence next to him. He was signaling his intention to move over into my lane! I honked my horn, but his engine was much too noisy for him to hear me. As he started to pull over into my lane, I honked the horn again but was eventually forced right off the highway. I slowed down on the sloping grass next to the road, kept control of the van, and then pulled back onto the highway. Later on, when the road leveled off again, I caught up with him and cranked it up to about eighty-five miles an hour in order to pass him quickly. I wasn't taking any more chances with his lane changes!

I seriously doubt that he was ever aware he had run us off the road. The interesting thing is that, just two hundred yards past the point where we were forced off the road, there was a guard rail. Had he pulled over at that point, there would have been no place for me to go. We would have been crushed against the guard rail or possibly even knocked over it and down the embankment. After this incident I finally told my wife about my impression of danger on the highway.

Her response was, "Well in that case we had better be *really* careful from now on."

But I responded, "No, it's over. That was what the Lord was trying to warn me about. Everything will be OK now." I was sensing a total release of anxiety that was just as real as the previous impression of danger. I somehow knew that the danger was past and that the rest of the trip would be reasonably uneventful. I was totally thankful for a God who cares enough and is able enough to give us advance warning about such things.

I do not wish to imply that God will always warn us or protect us. When bad things happen to God's people, it doesn't necessarily mean that they have done something wrong or are being punished. Ironically, on the way home from that very same appointment I was happily driving along through South Dakota with my speed control set at sixty-five miles per hour (the exact speed limit for that stretch of road). To this day I wonder why God gave me no advance warning about the policeman whose radar was calibrated (whether intentionally or unintentionally) at twelve miles over the actual speed. Though my speedometer said that I was traveling a steady sixty-five with speed control (that part of South Dakota is very flat), his radar machine said I was traveling seventy-seven miles per hour. And he had absolutely no sense of mercy. It turned out to be a very expensive traffic stop for me, even though I had obeyed the law completely, at least to the best of my knowledge. I plan to ask the Lord about this incident during the millennium. But if I have to choose, I would prefer to be warned about inattentive truckers than about mistaken or fund-raising policemen.

These incidents and others have led me to believe that God is very real and very down to earth. He is not fully consumed with running the universe; He would also like to be more involved in the day-to-day activities of our lives. And He seems to be just as willing to communicate with us today as He was with people back in Bible times.

Some words of caution

The idea that God would use impressions to communicate with us can be difficult for Adventists to accept, however. As Adventists we are leery of impressions. We fear the excesses of Pentecostalism, and with good reason. Charismatic Christians often seem to take their "spirit" far more seriously than they do the Scriptures. On one occasion I attended a Pentecostal church where the name of Jesus was used and much earnestness reigned, yet I could sense the presence of the demonic. It is possible for people to be praising God with their mouths and worshiping the devil at the same time without knowing it. So experience provides plenty of reason to be concerned about impressions.

Texts such as Galatians 1:8, 9 offer a significant balance to what we learn from the experience of Abraham.

> But even if we,
> or an angel from heaven,
> should preach a different gospel to you
> than the one we preached,
> let him be anathema.
> As I have already said before,
> and repeat again now,
> if anyone should preach a different gospel to you
> than the one you received,
> let him be anathema (Galatians 1:8, 9).

Paul implies here that impressions (like angels and preachers) can lead us contrary to the clear teachings of God. Satan can come to us in the guise of an angel of light (see 2 Corinthians 11:14, 15). No matter what the source, we should never accept an impression that leads us contrary to what we already know to be right.

After all, impressions can come from different sources. Impressions can come from God, designed to help us navigate through a variety of situations in life. But Satan can also give us impressions; we often call them temptations. Therefore, it's very important to be able to recognize whether God or Satan is speaking to us at a given time and place.

But many impressions come from neither God nor Satan. Some impressions may arise from the murky depths of our own inner selves.

Still others may reflect the expectations of other people. If we want to be attentive to God's inner voice, we need to be able to recognize the difference between these various kinds of impressions.

Regardless of whether they come from Satan, from some sort of inner fog, or from the expectations of others, impressions can lead us contrary to Scripture. With the exception of unusual circumstances such as that of Abraham, impressions should never supersede Scripture. Here is an illustration: One day a friend called me and said that he needed to see me. Since I had moved to another part of the country, he had to drive a considerable distance to meet with me. When he came, he had a woman with him who was not his wife. They were conservative Adventists. They wanted to do the right thing, but they had become convinced that each had married the wrong person and that God intended for them to be together in eternity. They had prayed about the situation and wanted to know whether it would be appropriate to exercise their "heavenly marriage rights" now or whether they needed to wait until they got to heaven to be married. I told them as kindly as I knew how that an impression to be unfaithful to your spouse is not from God. It's as simple as that. Impressions can lead you contrary to Scripture, but such impressions should be immediately discarded in nearly every situation.

Impressions can also lead you contrary to the way that God has made you. If a person with absolutely no stage presence felt impressed to become a comedian, I would be inclined to doubt that God was the source of that impression. If a person with no interest in details and few leadership skills felt impressed to become an administrator, I would question the source of the impression. If a motor mouth who can't read felt impressed to become a librarian, I would question the source of the impression. God has designed people in many different ways. We will be happiest and serve best when we are doing what God designed us to do.

Some people get energized by being with other people; others feel wiped out by the same kind of contact. When introverts have been subjected to a really major party, they usually have to go home afterward, pull the shades, and lie down in a dark room for a while to get their strength back. It breaks my heart to see people struggling to serve God in ways contrary to the way He "wired them up." So much energy is wasting merely "surviving." Beware of impressions that lead you contrary to the way God made you.

Impressions can also lead you into self-promoting and self-serving actions. You can feel impressed that tooting your own horn is the will of God. You may feel impressed that you have the absolute solution to some problem in the church. Yet in acting to resolve the problem, you may find out that you are simply exercising your own personal need for power and control. Destructive actions can seem very high and noble when they are backed up by strong impressions of doing the will of God.

Let us not, therefore, lose our sense of spiritual balance simply because Abraham had a very unusual experience with the voice of God. Impressions need to be handled with great care. The dangers that come along with impressions must not, however, cause us to lose out on the fantastic blessings that come from a living walk with God. For Christians living in a secular world there is no substitute for a living relationship with God. Such a relationship is the best safeguard against secular drift. Such a relationship is also vital to any outreach to secular people. Secular people have been "trained" to overlook God whenever they encounter Him in the church, on religious television, or in religious books. For many secular people, the only clear picture of God they will ever see is His living presence in another person's life. "Hearing God" makes Him real, not only to us, but also to those who have not known Him.

The "how to" of dealing with impressions

For our charismatic Christian friends the danger is placing feelings above the clear teachings of Scripture. On the other hand, many Adventists are so leery of emotional "experience" that they would rather live without any sense of God's presence than to risk making a mistake in judgment now and then. Here then is the challenge: How can we learn to know God's voice without falling into the pit of going contrary to Scripture or contrary to the way

God made us? I believe that there are some practical ways to accomplish this.

Allow me to expand on one of my prayer suggestions from the previous chapter. I noted that while we are accustomed to speaking to God in prayer, we rarely take the time to listen for His response. Try this process a few times. When you are ready to pray, take a pencil and paper with you. When you are finished, remain in position and wait quietly. Write down whatever thoughts and ideas come to your mind over the next five to ten minutes. This is sort of like spiritual brainstorming. When is God more likely to impress you with an idea than when you are already in an attitude of prayerful attention?

Now when I do this, I discover that a large percentage of the thoughts and ideas that pass through my mind are irrelevant to my life at that point. Some of them may be downright silly, as is fairly typical with any brainstorming process. But some of the thoughts that come to me are promising. I pass them through the filter of Scripture, as far as I understand it, and eliminate all ideas that are contrary to God's Word. What do I do with the rest? Test them and observe the results.

Whether or not an impression is from God can be discerned by the results of trying out the impressions that come to us. If you feel impressed to visit someone, visit them! If you feel impressed to make a phone call, make it! If you feel impressed to go shopping in a particular place, go there and see what happens. When you look back on your past experiences, you can often tell when God was leading and when you were going your own way. Reviewing your responses to various impressions, and the results that come about, can sharpen your sense of how God leads you personally.

Let's suppose that I feel impressed that certain people need to be contacted or prayed with. Suppose that when I contact these people they keep remarking about the exceptional timing of the contact or how badly they needed a visit right then. Suppose that wherever I go that day, people are blessed and the kingdom of God is advanced. This would suggest to me that God's hand was clearly behind the impressions that led me to do good at just the right time.

God has given me many days like that, and it feels so good! I am almost blown away by the sense of purpose and fulfillment. I get to know that there is a living God who cares enough to guide me in even the minor details of life.

But things don't always work out that way. Sometimes I feel impressed to make calls or visits—and the reaction is less positive. People may scratch their heads and have no idea why God might want me to contact them just then. The contact may even get me or them into trouble. Sometimes I feel impressed to do something special for a member of my family, only to discover that I have missed the mark widely! When the results of a particular impression do not work out for good, that impression likely came from a source other than God.

The key, then, is to try out your impressions, or at least the ones that aren't obviously stupid or contrary to the Bible. Experiment with them. Keep track of the results. Over time, you will gradually learn to distinguish the voice of God from some of the other voices in your head. You will find that God assumes a certain way of speaking with you, one that you gradually come to recognize and to trust. You may discover that His voice comes to you with a particular "accent." To gain this recognition will not come easily. It takes time and careful attention. But the joy that comes with God's leading is well worth the time and effort. God cares about the many areas of your life that are not directly governed by Scripture. And others are benefited by your sensitivity to Him as well.

On many occasions I've wanted to help someone but sensed that it might do more harm than good. For maximum effect, help must come at the right time, in the right place, and in the right way. Being sensitive to God's leading can make a major difference here. Scripture does not tell us whom or when to visit. God is willing to help us know when and how to approach people, but we need to be tuned in to His voice.

Ellen G. White states, "We have nothing to fear for the future except we forget how the Lord has led us in the past." Have you ever thought of extending this principle to your own life and experience? As you see how the Lord has led you in your own past, you will gain confidence to know that He will lead you also in the future. Perhaps I can share a couple of additional experiences from my own past in which I have been absolutely certain that God was leading me.

Finding the right one

One of the areas in which God's leading is critical is in the area of marriage. Many people venture into marriage "by faith" only to discover, often all too soon, that they made a big mistake. In my case, I looked for the right one all the way through college, but nothing permanent ever clicked. I was a pretty lonely guy when I graduated because I was leaving all the girls behind, and I was going out to pastor in an area where "little old ladies" were par for the course. The church to which I was assigned relegated me to the experience of four lonely walls at home and about fifteen elderly folk at prayer meeting. There was no real social life for a twenty-three-year-old.

My first interview with the conference president didn't help. For fifteen minutes he lectured me that he liked his pastors to be married. Then he changed course and warned me for another fifteen minutes that he didn't approve of ministers who dated! Go figure! By Friday of my first week things were pretty depressing.

On that Friday afternoon the senior pastor called and told me that he was giving a Bible study that night in a dangerous part of town. He said he wouldn't mind some company if I had some time free. Happy for a chance to get away from the lonely apartment, I agreed to meet him at his house at 6:00 P.M. On our way to the Bible study, he made a stop in a neighborhood that seemed different than the one he had told me about.

He said, "We have a little extra time, so I thought we could drop in on Pam for a few minutes."

"Who's Pam?"

"That's an interesting question. About two months ago she just walked off the street one Sabbath and announced that she had found the church in the phone book. She's been coming ever since, and I think she might be interested in being baptized soon."

So we went up to Pam's apartment and met her. She was in her late teens. She was dressed very casually, and at first sight I wasn't particularly impressed with her. When I saw her dressed up for church the next day, however, I was quite a bit more impressed. Three days later I was out visiting with the pastor again. He mentioned his plan of having a baptism that Sabbath, and he thought we should visit Pam again to find out whether she would like to be baptized as well. We were hardly seated in Pam's apartment when she took the lead in the conversation. "I hear that you're planning to have a baptism this Sabbath," she said.

"Yes, I think two or three young people are planning to be baptized," the pastor replied.

"Do you think there might be any room for me?" she asked.

Pastors, of course, live for moments like that. But then a strange thing happened (or maybe it's not so strange). On our way out of her place that day, we all shook hands, which is the pastoral custom. But there was electricity in that handshake for me. I didn't know what to do with that. It seemed entirely inappropriate for a pastor to feel excitement about a handshake. Months later she admitted that she had felt it too, and wondered if it was appropriate. In any case, I took note of the feeling, and our relationship began to grow. I offered her rides home from church. (I thought my little German sports car was cool, but she was into Mustangs back then.)

The senior pastor quickly discovered that he didn't have to take Pam home from church anymore. He wisely turned over her continuing Bible studies to me. On Sabbath afternoons we would find all the beautiful parks in New York City and spend time studying the Bible as well as getting to know each other. I'm very grateful that our relationship was centered on the spiritual when we started out. Before long we expanded our time together to include Sundays and a lot of late talking after prayer meeting on Wednesday nights (it's amazing that none of the old ladies got suspicious about this young lady who started attending prayer meeting after the assistant pastor arrived).

After a few weeks Pam decided to warn me about something. She told me that she had a long history of being interested in a guy for about two months, and then she would suddenly lose interest. I wasn't too worried, because things had gone really well up until then. After all, she was now a Christian, so things should be different. And anyway, I was different from all those other guys (the arrogance of youth)! But Christians are still people, and their personalities continue to be affected by their past experiences. Although God uses our unique personalities for Him, many quirks may continue after conversion. Sure enough, about two months into the relationship I sensed that something was missing.

We continued seeing each other, but the spark was clearly gone. I tried all the techniques of romance, from fancy restaurants to moonlight walks in the park. Nothing seemed to work. I was plagued with feelings of desperation, and I'm sure that it came through in the way I was acting. I loved her, and I couldn't bear the thought of losing her.

About that time she heard that her great-grandfather had died. She and her mom decided to go to the funeral back in the upper Midwest. Pam had grown up on a farm in North Dakota and had spent most of her life there. After her parents divorced, she eventually followed her mother to New York City. After a year or so in the big city, she longed for some token of home. She found it in church, which reminded her of the "safe haven" that church can provide for children in a mixed-up world. She never did like New York City very much and talked often about going back to the Midwest for college. So when she and her mom bought one-way plane tickets to North Dakota for the funeral (back then one-way tickets were cheaper than round-trip fares), I sensed that the relationship was over. At the airport, she said goodbye without any enthusiasm. I lamely offered my willingness to pay the fare back for both her and her mother, if they decided to return. Then I watched her go down the jet way and out of my life.

I went home to my four lonely walls—angry with God. When I had finally found the right one, He took her away. How dare He tease me like that, only to leave me more alone than ever! After a while, however, it dawned on me that my anger against God was not unanimous inside of me. I wasn't 100 percent mad at God; it was more like 80 percent. The other 20 percent of me thought that if a marriage to

Pam was not God's will, then it didn't really matter how fantastic she was. To marry someone outside the will of God could only be disastrous. And so a battle raged inside of me—80 percent of me wanted her back, no matter what the cost; the other 20 percent wanted to do God's will, no matter what the cost.

In spite of my offer to bring Pam and her mother back from North Dakota, several days went by without any word from her. My confused and jumbled prayers continued going up to God. A few days later it dawned on me that about 70 percent of me wanted her back, and 30 percent was saying that God's will was the thing that really mattered to me. After eight or nine days of silence, only 60 percent of me was saying that I wanted her back; 40 percent was praying for God's will to be done and for the help I needed to accept it.

I learned a very important lesson during that time. In the Christian walk we are often divided against ourselves. Our full devotion to God is undermined by a variety of voices within, some of which we may not even notice. But I learned that the human will can take hold of even the smallest kernel of faith, direct it toward God, and then, in turn, God will make that faith grow. Although the impression to place Pam's return in God's hands was my own, I knew it was the right impression even though most of me fought against it. When we place our will behind the impressions we know are from God, growth in character will take place, and our walk with God will become increasingly real.

It was the eleventh day. I was praying by my bed at about 11 o'clock at night (the two elevens make the timing easy to remember). In the middle of that prayer, I became aware that 51 percent of me wanted to obey God's will no matter what the cost. I told the Lord that even if I never saw Pam again it would be OK. Even if I needed to remain single for the rest of my life, it would be OK. I just wanted to do His will. An incredible sense of peace came over me. A sense of full, complete commitment. A sense that God approved of my decision. I knew that one way or another, everything was going to be all right. God was going to be with me, and He would take care of things.

You have to understand that my two previous relationships with women in college had ended in similar ways. In each case, someone I was interested in moved away for a while, something came up, and we never got back together again. For me, this experience with Pam was "three strikes and you're out"—a totally devastating experience. What a relief it was to resign the whole concept of a life partner into God's hands! My way wasn't working, anyway!

What comes next is not evangelistic exaggeration. I'm sharing with you exactly what took place. As I drew that 11:00 o'clock prayer to a close, I said in my mind, "In Jesus' name, Amen." At the very instant that the word "amen" passed through my mind, the phone rang. I got up from my knees, walked over to the phone, and picked it up. A voice said, "I have a collect call from Pam. Will you accept the charge?" First contact in eleven days! Pam said something about she and her mom needing to get back to the city and had I really promised to pay the fare? Well, needless to say, I was at the door of the local travel agency the minute the door opened the next morning. And I marveled at this incredible token of God's care for our relationship.

There have been days in our marriage when I've been tempted to say it was a mistake. (She's had those days too.) I thank God that I have a personal assurance that our marriage has His approval. He has chosen to use this relationship for better or for worse, for richer or poorer, to make me all that I can be for Him. I believe that sometimes God is just waiting to give us the desire of our hearts, but holds off because we demand it on our own terms. He waits until we are totally dedicated to Him, so that we will receive His gift in a beneficial way. At times our own selfishness may be the biggest obstacle to receiving the very thing we want most.

But there is one more piece to this story. When Pam came back from North Dakota, she didn't have any greater interest in me than she did when she left. She had needed a way back to New York, which she intended to repay. Then she would go on to a nearby Adventist college. We remained friends. But, in her mind, the romantic part of our relationship was over.

I was very confused. What did that 11:00 o'clock signal mean if it didn't mean God's approval for our eventual marriage? How could that marriage happen if one of us wasn't interested? Our summer ended outside a testing room at Atlantic Union College, where she was registering for studies. I was ready to drive back to New York and go on with my life. She was ready to take a test and get on with her life. We shook hands and said goodbye. I said, "It was a great summer; I will never forget you." I got into my car and drove away. And that was it. Or so it seemed. Thanks to my commitment to God, I was able to close the door and move on without further trauma.

When I got back to New York, I made arrangements to expand my ministry into areas that increased my social opportunities (such as teaching at the academy). I began looking forward to attending the Seminary the following year as an option by which God could open up the future. But above all I was content to go at His pace and in His place. Although I felt lonely at times, it felt great to be totally devoted to God.

Then one Saturday night, the phone rang. Once again an operator said, "I have a collect call from Pam; will you accept the charge?"

I indicated that I would.

"Hiiiiiiiiiiiiiiiiiiiiiiii!" said a bright, cheery voice on the other end of the line.

"Oh, it's you," I said somewhat matter-of-factly.

Pam had had time to think. She had had time to explore other options. She began thinking that she had lost something that she would later regret losing. She began feeling she had made a mistake in letting me go. She decided to call and see what was going on in my life. My reply made it clear that I had moved on and was not spending my days thinking about her. She was shocked. No guy had ever walked away from her before. They always got desperate when she pulled away, and that made her even less interested. Now it was her turn to be confused. Without planning it, she felt the attraction starting up again. Now it was her turn to get the fire between us rekindled. And she did a much better job than I did.

Over the next few months, phone calls and visits gradually rebuilt our relationship. Little by little we built a relational foundation that has lasted for decades. But we realize now that the key element was my willingness to let her go. And I could never have done that apart from my relationship with God. Only through a living relationship with God can we have the kind of detachment that truly loves another without keeping him or her in a cage. Our relationship could never have worked without a strong sensitivity to God's leading. But with God, all things are possible!

How to serve?

With regard to the issue of a life partner, a healthy experience with impressions is critical. When it comes to romance, feelings and impressions are extremely dangerous. Yet at no other time is a living relationship with God more vital to success. God's interest in human romance is clearly illustrated in the biblical stories about Isaac, Jacob, and Moses.

The second area where God's leading is absolutely vital is in the area of life work. The value of our lifelong service to God is enhanced when we discover His unique plan for us and how He has designed for us to succeed in carrying out His plan. I am grateful to God for His personal guidance in this area of my life as well.

After Pam and I got married, we went to the Seminary. Then I entered full-time into pastoral ministry. God blessed, and it seemed that a lifelong career in ministry was in view. But after a while, a number of little things suggested that I had not yet reached the place of ultimate service. People would say things like, "You're a good pastor, but have you ever considered teaching?" Or, "Your preaching is OK, but when you get a blackboard behind you and start a discussion going, that's when you really get on fire!" I found myself more excited in my personal study and in Sabbath School class than I was in the pulpit or doing visitation.

Then I heard about the biblical concept of spiritual gifts. I learned all I could about it and took a test. The test suggested three areas of major giftedness in my life: teaching, research, and missionary (the ability to relate to other cultures). As I pondered the possibilities, it seemed that the one place above all where I could exercise these gifts would be at the Seminary in Berrien Springs, Michigan. There I would be able to teach and have time for research, and I would be dealing with people from all over the world. If that wouldn't work out, another possibility would be to teach Bible in a college overseas.

One thing seemed clear, if God wanted me in higher education, I would need a doctorate. Since no one was offering to pay my way, Pam and I prayerfully decided to begin living sacrificially and saving all we could while continuing in ministry. When we had saved enough for a couple of years of study, we would move to Michigan, and she could earn the rest working as a secretary. But one thing we had always been committed to: When children would come along, she would be giving them her full-time attention. So we decided to postpone having children until after the doctorate was complete or at least until sufficient funds were available to take care of the educational costs.

When we reached our financial goals, we laid plans to move to Michigan. We informed the conference and our church that we would be leaving. We allowed the landlord to rent our house to other people. Pam found a good secretarial job at Andrews University, where I would be studying. We completed applications and entrance tests. Then, about a month before our move, came the big shock. Pam was pregnant. That meant that she would no longer be working after the baby's arrival. It also meant that most of her potential earnings would not be coming in. It meant that everything we had worked for was now in question.

I suggested to the conference that we could stay in our church for an extra couple of years to save more money for school. The conference and the church both welcomed the idea. But there was another problem. My landlord had already agreed to rent our house to someone else. But he was ecstatic when I told him that we wanted to stay (we were good friends). He said, "If that's the case, I will make it happen. I'm a lawyer. I have nothing down in writing with these people anyway. I'll just tell them they have to find another place." With that encouragement, I told the Lord that if we could stay in the same house and in the same church, it would be a sign for us to postpone the doctorate to another time.

When I saw Mike, my landlord, in his backyard the next day, his head was down and his hands were in his pockets. I went over to the low, chain-link fence that separated our yards. He told me that he loved us and wanted us to stay, but that he just couldn't break his agreement with the other people.

"Jon, I gave them my *word*," he said. "I just don't feel right about going back on my word."

I thought that if this secular lawyer was going to stand by his word and lose his good friend in the process, God must be behind it in some way.

I said, "Mike, you are the voice of God to me today." I could see he didn't know quite what to make of that, but he knew I thought it was a good thing. I told him that he was doing the right thing, and that I would try to do the same with my life. I knew that if God were leading, everything would work out, even if we didn't know where the money was going to come from. So Pam and I prepared to leave town.

Two days later, another friend of mine, who was president of a corporation, came to me and said, "You have some research skills that I could use. Would you be interested, while taking your doctorate, in being retained as a consultant for my corporation? I would send you a check for $300 every month and you could do some research for me from time to time, to help me in my business." My research interests and his expectations coincided, and the money he offered covered about half of what my wife would have been able to earn back then! The Lord was giving us a token: He would take care of things if we would only trust Him. As a result, we went to Michigan in faith, but with some evidence to support our faith.

Once God moved into action, one miracle chased another. During the first couple of years of my doctoral program, interest rates were at their highest levels for that century. This meant that for more than two years the interest on our savings, combined with the retainer, provided as much income as my wife would have earned had she been working. Then shortly after my arrival at the

Seminary, a General Conference Committee picked me, of all people, to do a major research project for which it was willing to pay a thousand dollars. A year after I arrived, the chairman of the New Testament Department told me that a professor who was on leave would be delayed for a quarter. Would I mind teaching the classes he would have taught? For a fee of course! For whatever reason, that professor kept delaying his return quarter after quarter. For two full years I was able to teach while studying nearly full time as well. The wages for contract teaching were small, but they looked big to me! And the experience was even more valuable than the money.

One day the Dean called me into his office. He said, "We appreciate what you are doing here a great deal. I've been going over your records, and I see that you have never received financial aid from us. Why haven't you asked?"

"I don't think I am eligible," I said. "You see, my wife and I like to know where our next meal is coming from, so we have chosen to do whatever it takes to keep up our cash position. Even though it would be nice to get financial aid, we are not in immediate need."

"We have to do something for you," he said. "Let me see. . . ." He picked up a thin book and began to leaf through it. "There must be a scholarship somewhere that is based on merit rather than on need."

That's the way God works when you are in the right place at the right time. I hadn't asked for help, yet the Dean called me in. I didn't think I qualified, yet he decided to find a way to make it happen. Over the next year he provided nearly $4,000 in merit scholarships! And that was only the beginning. The house we are living in also came to us under circumstances that are little short of a miracle, in timing, in cost, and in location. It couldn't have turned out better if we had planned it that way. A year later, when our money was about to run out, I was offered a permanent job at the Seminary. When I graduated, we did not owe anybody anything.

Nothing equals the feeling of knowing that we are where God wants us to be and doing what God wants us to do! And isn't that the kind of experience God wants for all who follow Him? I know that there are times when God doesn't choose to protect or to guide. There are times when God in His own purposes may not warn us of danger in advance. But when we see the love that sent Jesus to the cross, we know that we can trust Him no matter what the circumstances. There is no voice of guidance that can compare with His voice, whether in Scripture, the Spirit of Prophecy, impressions, or circumstances. This much I know. Whenever God is ready to speak to me, I want to be like Samuel and say, "Speak, Lord, your servant is listening."

CHAPTER

5

A LESSON FROM THE GULF WAR

In this chapter we continue examining the role of prayer in a living relationship with God. As we noted in the previous chapter, a Christian experience that will make a difference in the secular world will be conscious of God's presence and His leading in everyday life. But prayer can affect more than just individual lives. It can be a force that unleashes God's active power in the wider world context. In this chapter we will examine this wider significance of prayer and its influence on the larger events around us. The analogy that will help us to grasp the significance of this special category of prayer is based on military strategy.

Do you remember where you were and what you were doing when you heard that the Gulf War had started? I was at Walla Walla College, teaching an extension class for Andrews University to about thirty-five ministers. Along with teaching the class, I was expected to do some recruiting for the graduate programs of the Seminary. It was around 4:00 o'clock in the afternoon on January 15. I was interviewing a student when Ernie Bursey walked by the open door to the interview room. Ernie, one of the religion teachers at Walla Walla, is known for his opposition to war. As he walked by it seemed that his chin was dragging barely above his shoe tops.

"What's the matter, Ernie? You look terrible," I chirped.

"Haven't you heard?" he responded. "They just started bombing Baghdad a few minutes ago!"

A sense of numbness came over me as I felt the impact of what was actually taking place seven thousand miles away. I had lived through the Vietnam years, but the war in Vietnam had been different than this. Although Vietnam was a horrible experience for all who had to participate, the government and the media had always portrayed it as more of a police action or something like that. But the Gulf War was all-out war along the lines of World War II or the Korean conflict—a kind of warfare I had never experienced in my lifetime. Tens of thousands of Iraqi people, most of whom were totally innocent of Saddam Hussein's aggressions, would likely be dead by the time the war was over. Hundreds of thousands of my fellow Americans were facing a situation of unparalleled peril and stress.

Suddenly nothing else seemed to matter anymore. I couldn't wait to get back to my motel room and do exactly what Saddam Hussein was doing at that time—turn on CNN to figure out what on earth was going on.

The first piece of news to come was a huge shock. Military analysts had anticipated that the losses in an initial bombing attack on Iraq would be in excess of 10 percent of allied planes involved in the attack. Since 1,700 military aircraft were involved in the first attack, as many as 200 were likely to be shot down before Iraq's air defenses could be crippled. So the news that all but one of the planes in the first wave had returned safely to base was an enormous surprise. The success was not only beyond expectation, it was beyond the bounds of imagination. Losses at that level were unheard of in all the history of military aviation.

Right at that point I sensed that this war was going to have a much bigger impact on our perceptions of the world than I had expected. Along with most Americans, I waited eagerly for the Cheney-Powell briefing on the initial attack. It was scheduled for 9:00 P.M. Pacific time. I assumed that the first mission of the allied assault would be to take out the Iraqi air force and the military airfields.

But I was way off. When Cheney and Powell came to the podium, they were not talking about airfields or Iraqi aircraft at all. The primary focus of the attack was totally different. They said that the number one target of the initial air attacks in the Gulf War was "command and control." In fact command and control remained the primary target for several weeks. What on earth was that all about?

Command and control was not particularly concerned with the weapons that the Iraqis might use to contest an attack. Command and control had to do with lines of authority and communication within the Iraqi military and the wider Iraqi society. What Cheney and Powell were saying was that they weren't very afraid of the Iraqi aircraft or tank units. They were more concerned with the Iraqi ability to command and control their personnel and equipment, their ability to communicate.

Communication, not weapons systems, was the number one priority of the allied attack. This was like no other war I had ever heard of. And you know the result of that strategy. When the ground war started, it was no contest at all. All objectives were achieved in a matter of hours and with a minimum of losses.

Now this was anything but a given before the war started. You see, the Iraqis were much more competent than the results would seem to indicate. The Iraqi army was actually the fourth largest in the world at the time, and it was one of the best equipped. It had aircraft, tanks, and other weapons in large numbers and of high quality. Few countries could have done better against the kind of forces that were arrayed against Iraq on that occasion. The reason that the Iraqi army looked so pitiful and helpless was that it had lost communication—the ability to command and control that tremendous force. As a result, when the ground attack came, every Iraqi unit felt that it was fighting alone against an overwhelming force that was coming against it and it alone. It is no wonder that the Iraqi soldiers surrendered quickly in massive numbers.

A specific example of the power of communication in modern warfare was published in a *Newsweek* magazine article about six months after the war was over. It told the story of a commando team of three American soldiers that was air lifted about 160 miles deep into Iraq just before the war started. The goal of the commando team was to observe Iraqi movements and report back on the radio.

When it was dark, the commandos used night vision goggles to move around and make observations. As morning came, they would dig a hole in a good location for observation, get into it and cover it with vegetation for camouflage. They would stay in the hole quietly all day, then come out again at night and make more observations.

One morning they had located their observation post just outside an Iraqi village. Not long after daylight, one of the commandos became curious about what was going on outside the hole. This turned out to be a big mistake. As he lifted up one or two of the branches that provided camouflage, he found himself face-to-face with an Iraqi girl about seven years of age. His mind immediately went over the options available to him. The rules of engagement he was operating under required him to kill her on the spot and drag the body into the hole. Remaining undetected by the enemy was the highest priority of the mission. But as he looked into those young eyes, so full of life, he just couldn't do it. She might be an "enemy," but at that moment he also saw her humanity. He considered pulling her quickly into the enclosure, but even if he could keep her quiet, her absence would soon be noticed. So he tried a third option, to tell her in sign language that he was playing a game and that she was not to tell her father or anyone else that he was there. Then he let her go.

Of course, she went straight to her father and pointed out the location of the commandos. In a matter of moments, the foxhole containing three men was surrounded by a force of several hundred Iraqis. Bullets were flying all around, and heavier equipment was on its way. The situation of the three commandos appeared totally hopeless except for one thing—command and control. One of the commandos got on the radio and signaled desperately for help.

In Saudi Arabia, backup forces moved immediately into action. A heavily-armed Blackhawk helicopter rose from the ground in less than a minute and took off for Iraq at about 200 miles per hour, flying just a few feet off the ground to evade detection by Iraqi radar. In fact, the helicopter was flying so low that the pilot had to jerk it up into the air at one point to avoid a camel that happened to wander into its path! The Blackhawk arrived over the foxhole less than an hour after the girl had discovered it, and circled around the foxhole several times, spraying ammunition in all directions. It then quickly landed, and the three commandos jumped in and had a wild Disney ride all the way back to Saudi Arabia. When the helicopter arrived at home base, not one of the men was hurt.

That is a powerful example of the impact of what Cheney and Powell called "command and control." Communication is the key to modern warfare. The difference between the allied coalition and the Iraqis was the ability to communicate and coordinate forces at the decisive moment. As I read various reports after the Gulf War, I asked myself the question: Is there a spiritual lesson here somewhere? Can the Gulf War teach us to have a similar level of success in the Christian life? Is there a command and control aspect in Christian experience?

I turned to the New Testament, looking for answers. I discovered that warfare is a common biblical metaphor for the struggles that Christians experience in everyday life. It is also a metaphor for the kinds of challenges God's people will face during the final events of earth's history. A critical text is Revelation 16:14-16:

> For they are the spirits of demons
> doing signs,
> which go out to the kings of the whole inhabited world,
> to gather them for the battle
> of the great day of God almighty.
> Behold, I come as a thief.
> Blessed is the one who watches
> and keeps his garments
> in order that he might not walk naked
> and they see his shame.
> And he gathered them to the place
> which is called, in Hebrew,
> Harmagedon.

The word translated "battle" in verse 14 makes it clear that these verses employ military language. But notice verse 15, placed right in the middle of this passage!

> Behold, I come as a thief.
> Blessed is the one who watches
> and keeps his garments
> in order that he might not walk naked
> and they see his shame.

Elsewhere in the New Testament, these images—"the thief," "watching," and "keeping your clothes on" are used to illustrate spiritual readiness for the second coming of Jesus. So right in the middle of these Armageddon texts is a call for faithfulness to God. Revelation does not use military language to satisfy our curiosity regarding future political events. This glimpse of the future is given to prepare us to live right in the present! The battle of Armageddon is ultimately a spiritual battle. It is not about Russia and the United States or a battle for Middle Eastern oil. The battle of Armageddon is a battle between Christ and Satan for the allegiance of human minds.

The Christian's experience in the last days of earth's history, therefore, is described in military terms in the New Testament. This is even clearer when we read the statement of Paul found in 2 Corinthians 10:3-5:

> For though we walk in the flesh
> we do not make war according to the flesh–
> For the weapons of our warfare
> are not fleshly weapons
> rather they are powerful before God
> For the tearing down of strongholds–
> Tearing down arguments
> and every exalted thing
> that lifts itself up against the knowledge of God
> and making captive every thought
> to the obedience of Christ.

A Lesson From the Gulf War

Although not a part of Revelation, this is, in a sense, the clearest Armageddon text in all of the Bible. Christians have a warfare like the rest of the world has, but it is not a fleshly style of warfare. The weapons we fight with are not fleshly weapons. What are fleshly weapons? AK47 rifles are fleshly weapons. F14 fighter bombers are fleshly weapons. M1A1 tanks are fleshly weapons. What do these weapons do? They tear you to pieces. According to the New Testament, Christians don't fight with those kinds of weapons. The weapons we fight with are not fleshly weapons; on the contrary, they have divine power to demolish strongholds.

What kind of strongholds? Spiritual strongholds, not fleshly ones. According to Paul in 2 Corinthians, Christians have divine power to enable them to demolish arguments and all kinds of boastful pretensions that set themselves up against the knowledge of God. But even further, the Christian warfare is described as taking captive every thought and making it obedient to Christ. You see, the Christian warfare is a battle for the mind. A battle between supernatural forces that want to move us toward service of Christ or service of Satan. Have you had a battle for your mind going on this week? A battle over the thoughts in your mind? That's what Armageddon is all about. That's what Christian life is all about.

So the Bible uses warfare as one mental picture of Christian life. But Christian "warfare" is also very different from the "fleshly" kind. While warfare is a violent image, biblical warfare conquers by loving one's enemies, blessing those who curse us, praying for those who hurt us, and going the second mile when asked for a favor. Christian warfare overcomes evil in the way of Ghandi and Martin Luther King, not the way of Attila the Hun and Norman Schwartzkopf. True Christians bomb people with love and mercy, shoot grace at others, and shield themselves with authenticity and vulnerability. To use a common expression, Christian warfare is about "killing with kindness." This is crazy at first secular glance. But while the gospel's claims seem absurd at first glance, the Bible declares that the "weapons" of the gospel are more powerful than even the fleshly weapons of mass destruction and that they will have a greater impact on the course of human history!

How is this possible? How can the weakness of spiritual warfare be stronger than all the fleshly weapons of the human race? I believe, in the light of these Bible texts, that the events of the Gulf War can help us answer this question. The power of the allied attack did not lie in the explosive power of bombs or the shredding impact of bullets, but in a simple thing called command and control! Is there an analogy here that will open the way to the secret power of Christian faith? What is the command and control of Christian warfare? What is the crucial element that makes the difference between victory and defeat in the Christian life?

I have come to the conclusion that the best Christian analogy to the effect that command and control had on the Gulf War is nothing other than intercessory prayer. Intercessory prayer is when we intercede with God, not for ourselves, but in behalf of others. Intercessory prayer creates a chain of concern that links us not only to God, but also to each other. It is that aspect of Christian existence that most closely parallels the chain of command as well as the interlinked communications of modern warfare. And intercessory prayer is often misunderstood. We will cover three things about intercessory prayer in this chapter: (1) intercessory prayer works, (2) it is dangerous, and (3) it is good for us.

Intercessory prayer makes a difference

First of all, intercessory prayer works. It is not merely about the effect that my prayer has on me; it is very much about the effect it has on others. Intercessory prayer is based on the belief that my prayers can somehow make a difference in matters over which I have little or no control. This can be difficult to accept intellectually. Doesn't God already know the things I am praying about? Doesn't He want to intervene positively as much as or more than I want Him to? What difference could my prayer possibly make in the life of someone far away from me?

In spite of these difficulties, I have experienced powerful and unexplainable results from intercessory prayer, not just once or twice, but consistently over decades. I was once assigned to a church as pastor. Before I met with the congregation, I thought it would be helpful to get some feedback on the church from the previous pastor. I was not prepared for what he told me. He said, "This church is impossible to work with. You can do absolutely nothing for these people. Work on your car, get a lot of reading done; working with these people will get you nowhere." He went on to tell me, "I have never been able to preach more than ten minutes in this church. By the time I get that far, this incredible sense of darkness comes over me, and I just can't go on." He concluded, rather humorously, that the only thing that could be done for that church was to tie a cable around it, drag it out to sea, and then cut the cable.

I saw before me a broken and defeated man, slumped in his seat. As a young pastor, fresh out of seminary, I thought to myself, "Well, maybe he couldn't handle it, but he's not me. I'll show what can be done in circumstances like this!" So in confidence and stupidity I marched off that Sabbath to boldly preach my first sermon to that church. When I got up to preach, I instantly realized that he knew exactly what he was talking about. This was no game. There was a demonic presence in that Adventist church! I felt a choking sensation, and it seemed to be getting darker and darker.

The most incredible aspect of this experience was that there was an inch-thick plate glass completly dividing the pulpit from the congregation. So nothing I said was getting through. Now I know that the glass wasn't actually there, yet I could sense it fully as if it were. I looked through that glass to the congregation, and what I saw was bizarre. Children were climbing up over the back of the pews and underneath, then back out the front. Adults were talking to each other and paying no attention to me at all.

Nothing I said was getting through, and all the time I was feeling choked and sensed darkness coming over me. But all was not lost. My wife realized immediately that there were serious problems in the church that morning. She began to intercede with God for me and for the congregation, without my knowledge. About twenty-five minutes into the sermon, I heard a bell. The bell had a rather distinctive sound, somewhat like the mass bell in a Roman Catholic church. The instant I heard the sound of the bell, the glass that had separated me from the congregation vanished. Suddenly every eye in that church was wide open and fixed directly on me. The last few minutes of that sermon were as powerful as any other I have ever preached. Intercessory prayer works. I did nothing special on that day, but because my wife prayed, something very special happened.

A few years later, in Australia, a pastor and his wife came to me. They wanted me to pray with them for her healing from a terminal-type illness. I told them that I don't feel called to do that kind of thing as a rule, but that I was willing to try. I also decided to have the conference president join us because he knew the couple and he was a man of prayer. I was holding a series of meetings at the time along with Roland Hegstad, who was editor of *Liberty* magazine. We decided that he would preach while the rest of us met for prayer in a back room. We prayed. It felt special, but there was no immediate sign of healing.

When I came out on the platform, Elder Hegstad demanded to know what was going on in the back room. I asked him what he was talking about. He told me that in the previous hour he had experienced an incredible sense of the Lord's presence and power, such as he had never felt before in his life. It was as if a radiation were coming out of the back room. I was tempted to feel a bit of pride at the power of my prayers until I discovered that my wife had felt moved to pray at that very time back in the United States. Since that time I have learned to sense when my wife is praying for me even on the other side of the world. Her prayers in the United States that night (I guess it was the morning of the same day for her) made a powerful difference in Australia—a difference that others beside myself could sense. And perhaps most exciting of all, I met that pastor's wife again six years later, and she was doing much, much better! And she claimed that her turn for the better had started within a day of that prayer.

Some time after my experience in Australia, I was teaching an extension class at Walla Walla College; it was the same occasion referred to a bit earlier in this chapter. I did a really stupid thing on this occasion (not unusual for me). The plan the Seminary had laid out for me was to teach for five days, then spend five days recruiting theology seniors. But I didn't want to spend ten days away from home. I decided to do both things at the same time so I could get home earlier. That meant that I would teach every day from 8:00 in the morning until 3:30 in the afternoon. Then I would spend the rest of the day talking to the student prospects. When would I prepare for the classes? Oh, I figured I could squeeze that in here and there. Dumb idea!

Not only had I saddled myself with a nervous-breakdown level of responsibility, the Gulf War broke out right in the middle of it all. On top of all the stress related to my work was the concern about the world situation. By the time I came home, I had developed such an excruciating case of bursitis that I could hardly move for a week (that's the way my body often responds to overwhelming stress). I don't think, therefore, that I have ever taught a class when I was more tired, more distracted, or more unprepared. The amazing thing is that when the evaluations came in at the end of the week, I found out that I had never taught a class that was more highly regarded by the students!

What was going on? It certainly wasn't me. I was a wreck. When I arrived at home, I discovered that my wife and my daughter had hatched up a plot. The two of them felt impressed (although I hadn't said much) to get together throughout that week and pray for me at regular intervals. The results were far beyond any human calculation. Intercessory prayer makes a difference. We don't have to understand why to experience that difference.

My local church in Buchanan, Michigan has a custom every Sabbath of taking time to share joys, praises, sorrows, and requests. One year, without telling anyone, a psychologist in our church took notes on the various comments and tabulated them. In January, he surprised the church with his project and the results that he had discovered.

"Week after week, you do this," he said, "and you have no idea what is actually going on. I have been keeping track of every prayer request mentioned for the last year. Then I listen to see if anything happens. Do you realize that over the last year, 80 percent of all requests have been clearly answered in a positive way? We have got to take this part of the service even more seriously than we have. Your prayers make a difference. Your prayers are changing the world, whether you realize it or not!"

Clinically speaking, for our group at least, this was overwhelming evidence that intercessory prayer makes a difference. Since that time, I have become aware of scientific research that places this insight on an even stronger empirical basis. In 1995, Dwight Nelson reported to the Andrews University community the results of a "double-blind" study performed at San Francisco General Hospital and reported in the *Southern Medical Journal* (vol. 81, no. 7). For ten months, 393 heart patients in critical coronary care were randomly assigned to two different groups. Neither patients nor attending doctors knew which patient was in which group.

One group received normal scientific treatment for their conditions. The other group received the same treatment, and in addition was assigned to anonymous "intercessors," born-again Christian individuals who believed in and practiced intercessory prayer. All the intercessors knew about their assigned patients was their first name, diagnosis, and general condition. They prayed daily for a rapid recovery and for the prevention of complications and death. And when the study was over, those patients who had been prayed for, did significantly better medically than those patients who were not prayed for—in spite of the fact that neither group was aware of the experiment.

According to the article, those patients receiving prayer treatment "had less congestive heart failure, required less diuretic and antibiotic therapy, had fewer episodes of pneumonia, had fewer cardiac arrests, and were less frequently intubated and ventilated." You can question my own personal experiences all you want, after all, you shouldn't believe something just because someone else says so. But research studies utilizing significantly large groups are beginning to confirm what prayer warriors have suspected all along—intercessory prayer makes a difference, a big difference.

Don't ask me why. I know there are people who get very nervous about intercessory prayer, as if God is somehow being compelled to do something in other people's lives. Intercessory prayer may not be logical. I don't understand why it works, but I know that it does. And the Bible clearly supports its validity. I think of 1 Timothy 2:1, 2, where the apostle clearly urges believers to pray for "kings" and all those in authority, many of whom we will never influence personally. And Paul expects those prayers to make a difference. He says we should pray for these officials "that we may live peaceful and quiet lives in all godliness and holiness" (1 Timothy 2:2, NIV). I also think of Daniel 10, where one man's prayers succeeded in turning around the course of a superpower nation.

I'm not sure why things like that happen, but I know that they do happen! Somehow, in the course of a great controversy between light and darkness, the free-will intercessions of moral agents like ourselves provide a context in which God can act against Satan with an authority that would not otherwise be possible. This is clearly not because God is unable or unwilling apart from our prayers. But somehow our prayers change the circumstances in which God works. Dwight Nelson offered a suggestion, "Maybe in the great battle for human allegiance, the forces of light and darkness have somehow mutually bound themselves to the rules of fair play. Could it be that our intercessory prayers actually provide God with permission to intervene with power and love in the life of someone else who is being victimized by the forces of evil, someone else who does not have the presence of mind or the strength of faith to solicit God himself?" (*Andrews University Student Movement*, January 10, 1995, p. 11) Whether or not we buy that particular suggestion, the results of intercessory prayer are worthy of our attention.

Intercessory prayer can be dangerous

While there is abundant evidence that intercessory prayer works, there is also evidence that it is dangerous. It seems to increase the vigor of Satan's attacks against us personally. Satan is a defeated foe, but he can certainly be irritating at the least, and frighteningly dangerous at the worst. Let me clarify this complex dynamic with another illustration from the realm of military action.

Unlike the Gulf War, which was characterized by mass military movements along the lines of World War II, the war in Vietnam was fought, to a large degree, by relatively small units. Typically, a dozen or so men would leave their base to go out on patrol, searching for small units of the enemy. Normally, all of the men were heavily armed except one, the radio man. He would be lightly armed because he had to carry a heavy pack containing the equipment for radio communications.

Veterans tell me that when the enemy came along and saw the patrol, they rarely fired first at the most heavily armed members of the patrol. They went after the radio man first, if they could identify him. They did this because they knew that the radio man was the key to the skirmish. What could the radio man do without heavy weapons of his own? More than anyone else on that battlefield. With a simple call on the radio, he could totally change the odds.

If the patrol found itself faced with a regiment of more than a thousand men, for example, the radio man would immediately go into action. He could call in an air strike by helicopters or heavily-armored "tank-killer" aircraft. He could call for an artillery strike from heavy howitzers, giving exact locations to ensure accuracy. He could arrange for massive reinforcements of personnel and equipment. He could suggest a helicopter airlift or an air drop by paratroopers to surround the enemy by surprise. In other words, all by himself the radio man could bring decisive numbers to the decisive point of the battle. He was as valuable as any general in the type of engagement that was typical for Vietnam. It is no wonder that the job of radio man was so dangerous. The enemy feared him more than it feared anyone else!

But there were even more reasons for the enemy to be concerned. Communication is a two-way street. The radio man could do more than just call for help, he could also operate as forward intelligence. He could detect enemy signals and communications. He could answer questions about the battle situation that would affect the decisions made by the officers back in camp. He could find out exactly where the enemy was and pass that information along. He could determine how strong the enemy was and what kind of attack was coming. The radio man was the key to keeping the commanders in control of the situation. At the point of battle, he was better than a hundred spies without the ability to communicate quickly. No wonder it was so dangerous to carry the radio! In guerrilla warfare, silence and secrecy are crucial. The radio man had the capacity to undermine the operations of the enemy all by himself in ways that no one else could.

Just as in the Gulf War, the key was command and control. The commanders needed "intelligence"; their decisions depended on knowing exactly what was going on at ground level. In today's world, this information is increasingly obtained from satellites. But during the Vietnam War, the radio man in the field was the decisive figure in most small engagements. "Intelligence" makes the difference between success and failure in many a battle.

I remember when President Reagan was in his first year of office. He complained one day that his work was greatly hampered by his predecessor's decision to downsize the Central Intelligence Agency, America's best-known spy agency. In one of his early speeches, he made the kind of self-effacing verbal slip for which he was beloved: "Ever since I became president, there has been a serious lack of intelligence in the White House!" Commanders need good information in order to make the right decisions. The result of effective communication in battle is victory, even when the situation of the units in place would suggest defeat.

Like military communications, Christian command and control has two sides. One side is intercessory prayer, the sending out of calls for help. But on the other side is sensing what God is saying back to us. Intercessory prayer provides the network of encouragement and support that empowers the Commander's actions in the field. Impressions are a major way our Commander-in-Chief guides the troops.

But there is a dark side to this reality. The command and control of Christian warfare is as perilous a mission as was the role of the radio man in Vietnam. My wife can tell you of times when she herself has felt the attack of Satan in the context of intercessory prayer. Just as Satan did all he could to destroy Daniel's prayers for his people (the lions' den story occurs around the same time as Daniel's mighty prayer of intercession for Israel—compare Daniel 5:31;6 with Daniel 9:1-19), so he devotes similar attention to those who are making a difference in prayer today. He will do all he can to assault intercessors with fears, random physical pains, and sometimes direct manifestations of his presence. If he can get people to stop praying, the battle is largely won. But although intercessory prayer creates complications for those who exercise it, command and control is the key to victory. We must not allow ourselves to be deterred from the very thing that makes the decisive difference in so many spiritual engagements.

Intercessory prayer is good for us

The previous sections of this chapter suggest that while intercessory prayer does great things for other people, it comes at a high cost to the one who prays. Prayer can be difficult enough to sustain when one has a vending-machine view of God. If intercessory prayer brings us negative attention from Satan, we may feel that it is not worth the cost to us. But there is a third dimension to intercessory prayer that counterbalances the spiritual danger that comes in the context of prayer for others. Intercessory prayer is not only beneficial for others, it is very beneficial also to those who pray. There are a number of reasons for this.

For one thing, when we pray for others, it changes our attitude toward these individuals. It is certainly difficult to maintain hard feelings toward someone for whom you are praying every day. When we seek God for good in behalf of those who have rejected Him, the Spirit of God draws near and brings us a taste of the infinite love of God for such souls. When we seek God in behalf of those who dislike us, we receive a taste of His love for those who dislike Him. As we come in touch with God's attitude toward the lost, our own attitude begins to change. Prayer for others changes us.

There are other benefits to those who pray. When we pray for others, we ourselves receive in kind. When we pray that someone else should come to Christ and be forgiven, we become more able to sense our own forgiveness before God. As we learn to pray for people who have hurt us, we ourselves can experience forgiveness for the times we have hurt others. When we pray for others, our own relationship with God grows. The two things seem to work together; if we pray for others, we ourselves are blessed.

Another benefit of intercessory prayer is that when we pray

for others we become more and more like Jesus, who prayed for His enemies as well as for us. And by praying for us, Jesus has set an example that we should pray for one another. As we pray for one another, we develop a deeper relationship with the Lord and gain a deeper appreciation of His concerns for others and their situations.

Perhaps most important, intercessory prayer can give us a tremendous sense of fulfillment as we realize that something we are doing is making a difference in the world. One of the deepest human needs in every generation is the need for fulfillment in life, for some way to make a difference. Intercessory prayer is one of the most powerful ways to make a difference. Let me share an example with you.

A few years ago I decided, while traveling in another part of the country, to make a phone call to the pastor who had baptized me when I was twelve years old. As a kid, I had always been in awe of him. He was such a man of God. I saw in him a model of what I might become if I would go into ministry. He was always earnest and serious, but there was a quiet friendliness about him toward children that always attracted me to him. By the time I decided to call him, he was retired, in his 80s, and living near the place were I was staying. I placed the phone call, not knowing what to expect. When I connected with him, I asked him what he was doing with his life. I was totally unprepared for his answer.

"Nothing! I do nothing!" he said. "I do nothing; I am nothing; I am like garbage! Every day I just sit around and do nothing, just waiting for tomorrow to come. Sometimes I go out into the garden for a half an hour or so, but otherwise I just sit and do nothing. I wait for the Lord to take me home and give me rest."

I was stunned. I didn't know what to say. I sent up a quick prayer asking for guidance and then caught an idea. I asked him if he still prayed.

"Yes, of course," he said.

I asked him if he knew that intercessory prayer makes a difference.

"Yes, I suppose so," he said.

I asked him to pray for me and my ministry wherever I go. I shared how much the prayers of others had made a difference in my ministry. I told him that while his body wasn't capable of doing much for the Lord any more, he could still make a major difference. He could pray for the General Conference, the Lord knows they could use all the help they can get! He could pray for his conference president. I told him that the administrators of the church were very busy people. They love the Lord and know how important it is to pray for the work in their areas, but they are extremely busy. They don't have time to pray as much as they would like. But he had time to pray. Perhaps God was keeping him alive because He needed individuals who would take the time to pray for His cause in that area.

I shared with him some of the things you have read in this chapter, of how intercessory prayer made a difference at various points in my experience. An amazing thing happened. As the phone call went on, I began to detect a smile creeping into his voice. Then he became more and more excited, and a sense of hope began to arise in force. He began to believe that the Lord was giving him time so that he could pray.

"It is easy when you get old to feel as if your best days are behind you," I said, "but if God has kept you alive this far, maybe it is because your greatest days are still ahead of you! Maybe your conference has been dying for lack of the prayers that only you can pray. Maybe you are the key to the work of God in this area, and you don't know it!"

By the time that phone call was over, he was on fire to live. He was no longer waiting for the Lord to take him home. The Lord was already with him in his home. His life now had a mission and a purpose. What a difference the concept of intercessory prayer can make! Perhaps you are also "over the hill." I know that I am not so far away myself. Like my former pastor, I also wonder sometimes what difference I am making in this life. I also wonder if my best days are behind me. I too forget that there's a way to make a massive difference in this life. It isn't the weapons that we carry that make the difference in spiritual warfare; it's the command and control that wins the battle.

Barriers to prayer life

If intercessory prayer is the key to spiritual victory, why do we do so little of it? Is it because really deep down inside we have a secular mentality? Do we somehow believe that prayer is a waste of time, that it doesn't really make a difference? Or is the problem that we are essentially self-sufficient? Do we feel that in spite of the claims of the Bible, God is not really plugged into what is happening in this world, and so nothing is going to get done unless we do it? Ask the Iraqis how well self-reliance works.

Do we neglect intercessory prayer primarily because we are forgetful? We intend to pray but we just forget? Do we get distracted like small children in spite of our vow that we are going to spend more time in prayer? Or is it the tyranny of the urgent? "Yes, I will pray as soon as there is a little bit of time. I'm a little busy right now, but next week I'll start. I know I should pray, but I have this deadline tomorrow, and prayer will just have to wait." How can we change those ingrained habits of letting intercessory prayer be the last and the least?

It seems to me that intercessory prayer is the place, above all others, where we become exposed to our own secularity. What is the point of praying for others if we don't believe it will make any difference? What is the point of praying for others if we are not sure whether God is real? Any desire we may have to reach out to the secular people in our world will ultimately fail unless our compassion finds expression in prayer for them. I myself have stumbled in this area many times, but over the years I have learned a few strategies that have helped.

Getting our prayer act together

The first thing that will make a difference in the area of intercessory prayer is to set a regular time for prayer. This may seem rather elementary, but it is crucial. Set a specific time for intercessory prayer, if possible the very same time each day. One of the best spiritual disciplines is to develop a habit of prayer. Habits develop out of regularity and repetition. When you do something over and over every day, it eventually becomes a habit. When things become a habit, they become much easier to do.

A second suggestion is to make a prayer list, but to avoid some of the pitfalls in list-making. Most people make the mistake of putting together a long list of the names for which they would like to pray. Long lists are easy to do. People love to have others pray for them, and it is not comfortable to decline such a request. But the plain reality is that long lists are exhausting for most people, and the end result is often that the list exists, but gets very little attention. After a while, praying over a long list becomes too much work for most people.

I would suggest, therefore, keeping the list short, at least to start with. Three names is probably enough, especially if you have never succeeded at intercessory prayer for long. At the top of the list, I would suggest putting the most difficult person you know. I'm talking about the person who bugs you more than anybody else. The person who makes your stomach churn whenever he is around. The person who doesn't take your feelings and needs into account. The person who blasts through your life like a steamroller crushing everything in its path. Hopefully I'm not talking about your boss or your spouse here.

There is nothing arrogant about recognizing the negative impact that some people have in your life. Some of it is related to clashing personalities. Much of it may be beyond the awareness of the other person. No doubt you are at the top of somebody else's list, so it's smart to be humble about this! But God wants us to have the experience of praying for difficult people, just as Jesus did for His disciples (see John 17). An amazing thing happens when you pray for someone who is difficult. Over time, it changes your feelings about that person. As you view him or her through God's eyes, you see value and possibilities that you didn't see before.

Along with the name at the top of your list, put down a couple of more promising names. Seeing some results right away is extremely encouraging. When things change in the lives of the people you are praying for, you may want to replace one or more people on your list with someone else who is in greater immediate need. Some may prefer to have a second list, a longer one, that gets attention from time to time. But the primary list should be relatively short and manageable.

The most important aid to a consistent prayer life, finally, is accountability. Very few people accomplish anything in life without accountability. If you want to succeed at an exercise program, for example, there's nothing better than having a friend meet you at a particular time and place and jog or work out with you. The key to the battle is often how you answer your alarm in the morning. The bed is so inviting, and the exercise seems so difficult. But then you remember that your friend will be waiting for you in ten minutes. That gets you up when nothing else will. And it doesn't even matter that the friend would probably not have made it either if *you* hadn't promised to be there! Accountability can replace weak spots in our will power with just enough steel to get the job done. And the result is a benefit to both parties!

How does accountability work in relation to intercessory prayer? There are several possibilities; I will mention three. One type of accountability is to meet regularly with a group for prayer—a set time and a set place for prayer with people you care about. The downside of such a group lies in the area of gossip and confidentiality. Groups can sometimes lose their focus on the main task. But the upside of a group is the variety of styles and interests resident in a gathering of people with a common concern. This can keep the prayer focus from getting into a rut or seeming stale.

Another type of accountability occurs when you team up one-on-one with a prayer partner. Meeting together regularly provides accountability to the task. There is a special bonding that takes place between two people in a common relationship with the Lord. Since there are only two of you, there is less chance that the prayer time will digress into gossip or side issues. You can come to know each other well enough to take the accountability to a deeper level than is possible in most groups.

But a regular meeting with one or more friends doesn't work out for everyone. In some cases the best kind of accountability is to have an understanding with a hard-nosed friend. I have a few hard-nosed friends, and I thank God for them. What do I mean by hard-nosed friend? The kind of friend who cares enough about you to confront you when you need it. Suppose you tell a friend that you plan to spend fifteen minutes—from 7:00 to 7:15—every morning in intercessory prayer. You ask that person to hold you accountable to do that. A hard-nosed friend is someone who calls at 7:17 in the morning to check whether you did or not! That kind of friend can make a big difference in your prayer life. All three forms of accountability can help us maintain the kind of consistency we long to have.

Prayer can move mountains

In the book *The Master's Plan of Prayer* (p. 186), the story is told about the aftermath of the Rodney King beating and the subsequent trial of the police officers involved. Rioting broke out in Los Angeles during April 1992. New York City anticipated similar troubles. TV news crews were prepared to cover the story. But instead of riots, news teams found people all over the city praying.

It seems that a month before the riots began in Los Angeles, a number of New York City pastors felt a strong urge to begin a prayer offensive in behalf of the city. Churches began opening nightly, and as many as a thousand persons attended, praying for the city's needs. People prayed for the poor, prayed for racial harmony, prayed for God's protection in behalf of New York. The day after the L.A. riots broke out, a weekend of eight Community Concerts of Prayer involved three hundred metro churches. And instead of rioting, calm prevailed.

There may have been an even greater and more long-term result than those originally involved were aware of. An amazing drop in crime statistics over the last decade has made New York City one of the safest places in the country. I experienced the new atmosphere in the city myself this summer, returning after eighteen years. I saw many women walking alone at night, something that occurred rarely when I lived there in the '60s and '70s. The change was remarkable.

Many have attributed the changes in New York City to the mayor and a new philosophy of crime fighting. But recent events demonstrate that New York City police make mistakes, just like the police in Los Angeles do. Others have cited demographic trends as the reason for the changes. But these same trends have not had such a stunning effect in Chicago or L.A. as they have had in New York. Both factors have no doubt played their part. But isn't it equally possible that a city-wide commitment to prayer can have as great an impact in driving back the forces of evil as do police and demographics? Perhaps the city that prays together stays together! Why should God's command and control be any less effective than Colin Powell's?

More and more I have come to believe that my life and ministry would be a total waste if no one prayed for me. God has given me many talents, yet I have less and less confidence in my abilities as the years go by. I see more and more that prayer is the key that opens spiritual doors and moves spiritual mountains. Since that is true, I am one of the luckiest men on earth because I have a wife who prays for me when I need it most. Along with her, there are many other people on six continents who have made a decision on their part to pray for me and my ministry, and I can only begin to imagine the kind of difference that makes.

You may want to consider the possibility that God is calling you to be a key player on His command and control team.

CHAPTER
6

ARE YOU FOR REAL?

In this concluding chapter, we will probe what I consider to be the ultimate issue of Christian faith in the real world: Does it make a difference most people would notice? Is it a genuine expression of reality or is it an escape from reality, an "opiate of the people"? What does it mean to be a *real* Christian? What does it mean to be authentic or genuine? We are all familiar with the concept of "psychological masks," a person trying to show himself to be something he is not. This can be especially tempting when you are a Christian among Christians, because everybody knows what kind of behavior is expected. If you don't feel very "Christian" that day, it is very easy to put out the appropriate signals without really meaning it. But phony Christianity does great harm in the secular world.

If you had asked me thirty years ago whether I was a "real Christian," I would have had no trouble answering, "Absolutely! What you see is what you get. I'm the ultimate straight shooter." And I would have been wrong.

I was visiting the Riverside Church in New York City one Sunday with a couple of friends. Riverside Church has one of the five largest classical organs in the world. Being an organist myself, I never got enough of it. The organist that day was Frederick Swann. He was internationally famous, with dozens of recordings. And he played magnificently that Sunday morning.

KNOWING GOD IN THE REAL WORLD

When the worship service was over, I took my friends up on the platform to get a closer look at the organ. And since I knew quite a bit about such things, I began to explain some of the different features of the organ. As I talked, the audience began to grow. It was fun! So I began to expand on the story a little. And the audience got even bigger. Then suddenly I began to realize that the people weren't looking at me anymore. They were looking behind me. I turned around and was standing face-to-face with Frederick Swann. He looked me in the eye and said, "You'd better get your facts straight, Sonny, before you open your mouth." Then he turned and walked away. Have you ever wished the ground would open up and swallow you? I learned a very painful lesson in authenticity that day.

Honestly, now, are you for real? Are you really the person you seem to be? If you had asked me that question twenty-five years ago, I would have said, "Absolutely. What you see is what you get." But even then, I doubt that the evidence would back me up!

You see, I was just starting out in ministry. And a strange thing seemed to happen. Every Sabbath I would get a big headache. It would start in the middle of Sabbath School and last until the middle of the afternoon. I couldn't understand why. After a year or so, the Lord finally revealed to me what the problem was. The problem was that I was trying to be someone that I was not. I was trying to be the kind of pastor I thought everyone wanted me to be. And it was making me sick. Then the Lord passed on this message to my mind, "I didn't ask you to be Billy Graham. I didn't ask you to be H.M.S. Richards. I didn't ask you to be George Vandeman. All I want is for you to be Jon Paulien. And do that for Me."

What a relief!

Honestly, now, are you for real? Are you really the person you seem to be? If you had asked me that question ten years ago, I would have said, "Absolutely. What you see is what you get. I'm the ultimate straight shooter." But again, I doubt that the evidence would have backed me up!

About ten years ago, I heard a particular preacher for the first time. He had an incredible impact on me. Whenever he spoke, my heart would burn within me. It was as if he could read my soul. It was similar to the way I sometimes feel when reading Ellen White. But he was not a prophet. He made that very, very clear. He was just an ordinary Christian, speaking from the heart. And yet his words had prophetic power.

What was it that made his preaching so powerful? Ninety percent of his illustrations were from his own personal experience. And when he offered illustrations from his own experience, he almost always talked about his failures—not his successes. That led me to think about my own sermons. And I began to realize that when I gave illustrations from my own personal experience, I always talked about my successes. I almost never talked about my failures. So even ten years ago, I came to realize that I was still using the pulpit to polish my image.

A new look at Laodicea

Honestly, now, are you for real? Are you really the person you seem to be? A few years ago I was sitting in a restaurant with several of the leaders of the Seventh-day Adventist Church in North America. In the middle of lunch, one of them turned to me and said, "Jon, what do you think is the greatest need of the Seventh-day Adventist Church today?"

It was probably because of this history of mine—this journey toward becoming real—that I responded the way I did. "Oh, probably to stop living a lie," I responded quickly.

At first my own answer puzzled me. But the more I thought about what I had said, the more sense it made. I believe that one of the great challenges we face as a Church is the challenge to stop trying to put on a show for the world. To stop trying to act as if we were perfect, and instead seek to be honest and open regarding our faith.

But don't take my word for it. Just ask Jesus what the greatest need of the Adventist Church is. He has told us in plain terms in Revelation 3, in the message to the church of Laodicea. There Jesus brings His message home to His end-time church. Notice His words in verse 17:

Laodicea

Rev 3

"You say, 'I am rich;
I have acquired wealth
and do not need a thing.'
But you do not realize
that you are wretched, pitiful, poor, blind and naked" (NIV).

Problem

According to this text, what is Laodicea's problem? The problem is that what Laodicea says she is and who she actually is are two different things. Laodicea has put on a mask of riches, but she lives in a reality of poverty. She's put on a mask of beautiful clothing, but she is living in the reality of nakedness. She claims to be living on easy street, but she is actually wretched and homeless. What does she need? Notice verse 18:

"I counsel you to buy from me
gold refined in the fire,
so you can become rich;
and white clothes to wear,
so you can cover your shameful nakedness;
and salve to put on your eyes,
so you can see" (NIV).

Cure

I want to focus particularly on the last part of verse 18, the problem of spiritual blindness. The answer to Laodicea's problem is medicine for the eyes so that her vision will become clear. Laodicea is living in a spiritual fantasy world. Her self-image is totally unrelated to Jesus' opinion of her, totally unrelated to ultimate reality. He offers to give her what she does not have—a clear perception of her condition.

Jesus sums up in verse 19: " 'Those whom I love I rebuke and discipline. So be earnest, and repent.' " Jesus speaks this message, not because He hates Laodicea, but because He loves her. And He wants to give her this message so that she can be healed and be real again.

In these verses, Jesus identifies a two-fold problem. First, Laodicea needs to repent of her phoniness, her lack of authenticity. Without such repentance, she will never be what Jesus desires of her. But the second problem is even more serious; she doesn't even know she is faking it! She is totally unaware that her spiritual claims are bogus!

In applying this text to the current situation in the Adventist Church, I am not pointing the finger at others. For one thing, *Jesus*, not me, is the One passing judgment here. And for another thing, it would be inappropriate for me to accuse others of something I am guilty of myself. My whole history is a history of being something I'm not. So please understand, the problem of not being authentic is not just *your* problem or *the Church's* problem; it is *our* problem; it is *my* problem.

I know that this problem is not limited to North America. Wherever I go, people come up to me and say, "There are things going on here that I want to tell you about because you are from another country. If I say these things here, people will use them against me. If I talk to you, I can speak freely." This is the great fear of Laodicea. We are afraid that if we reveal who we really are, people will turn against us.

The struggle to be real

What does it mean to be real? Being real is when the outside and the inside are the same. It is when the things we reveal about ourselves are in accord with the real truth about ourselves. This problem of "inside vs. outside" was familiar to the apostle Paul:

> For our appeal
> does not arise out of deception
> or out of uncleanness,
> or out of some kind of trick.
> On the contrary,
> just as we were approved by God
> to be entrusted with the gospel
> so we speak
> not to please people
> but rather to please God,
> who tests our hearts.
> For we never came to you

> with a word of flattery,
> as you know,
> nor on a pretext of greed;
> God is witness,
> nor did we seek glory from other people,
> not from you
> and not from anyone else (1 Thessalonians 2:3-6).

Apparently, Paul was responding to an accusation attacking his inner motives. He was accused of being a phony. And he agrees with his opponents that ministry is not immune to this problem. A person can enter ministry for a lot of reasons. A person may enter ministry because he thinks it is glorious to stand up in front of people. He may enter ministry to gain money. According to Paul, some may even enter ministry to gain sexual advantage (that's the implication of the word *uncleanness* in verse 3)! Paul is certainly not dancing around the issue in these verses.

Paul speaks to the need for pure motives, not just pure actions. In the Greek, this passage is even more frank than it is in translation. Paul speaks directly of sexual motives, of financial motives, and of motives of glory and praise. There are a lot of reasons why a person might choose to serve the Lord, and many of them are not spiritually healthy. What scares me most, however, is that those of us in ministry may not even be aware of some of these deeper motives. It is easy to fake it. It is natural to put on a mask.

I remember a friend in school—one of those rebellious types. He would always park his car in the handicapped parking spot or in front of the garbage dumpster. He would sit in the back of the class and throw balled-up bits of paper around and generally thumb his nose at Church authority. Years later he was a student in a doctoral class that I was teaching. He sat, all slouched down, in the very last row. And almost every day he would raise his hand and talk about "them" and how "they" were ruining the Church. He was speaking about Church administrators.

Finally, one day I stopped him. I said, "You know what? 'Them' is 'us.'"

The Suit

It just happened that three conference presidents and five union presidents were in that class. So I said to this individual, "Those who hold a doctorate in ministry degree will be the leaders of the Church tomorrow. What are you going to do if 'they' make you president of a conference?"

What happened next was truly ironic. Three weeks after the class ended, I got a phone call from this person. He had just been elected vice-president of one of the largest conferences in North America. I said to him, "Here is your chance to demonstrate that you can do it better."

And he must have done well. A few years later he became a conference president in another area. I was interested to find out how he was surviving among "them." One day I noticed that we had been assigned to the same General Conference committee. We would be together that day. I entered the room and saw him on the opposite side. I came rushing over, planning to give him our usual "high-five." Then he turned around to face me. He was wearing a three-piece suit, and his elbow seemed attached to his side. He held out his hand in a dignified manner and said in a quiet voice, "Hello, Jon. So nice to see you again." I was shocked! In a matter of three years he had become one of "them"!

Now don't get me wrong; he's a really great guy. But this experience reminds me that it is totally natural to try to live up to the image that people have of us. It's human to want others to think well of us. It's hard *not* to change when you find yourself in a position of some importance. It's natural to try to build a sense of self-worth through performance, image-making, and the praise of others. The good news is that my friend is finding himself again. I've heard that he is beginning to set a trend toward a more open and honest style of leadership. But there is no question that it was a great struggle for him. I know, because I am no different. It's natural for us to try to be someone we're not.

Why is it so natural? Because we are afraid to be real. We are afraid to show our true selves. We are afraid of what other people might think. We're afraid of how they'll respond to us. That's nothing new; the same thing happened in Jesus' day. Notice John 12:42, 43.

Even among the priests
many believed in Him,
but because of the Pharisees
they would not confess it
In order that they might not be thrown out of the synagogue;
for they loved the glory of men
more than the glory of God.

According to the Gospel of John, if we do the things we do because we love the praise of other people, we will not be doing the things that give glory to God. Jesus goes even deeper in John 3:20 (NIV). " 'For Everyone who does evil hates the light, and will not come to the light for fear that his deads, might be exposed.' " Apparently there is something really scary about letting our true selves show. Just ask me. I've had plenty of experience!

Defense mechanisms

Why is it so hard to be real? Why is it so hard to be authentic? There is a whole division of psychology related to what are known as defense mechanisms. It seems that human beings have built-in mechanisms of defense. They kick in the minute we're under pressure emotionally or psychologically.

Let me illustrate how defense mechanisms work. Let's suppose I am teaching in a large classroom one day. Then Randy Johnson walks in the back door of the classroom with a baseball in his hand. For those who have never heard of Randy Johnson, let me just say that he is six-foot-ten and can throw a baseball 101 miles per hour with his left hand! Let's suppose that Randy takes exception to something I tell the class and launches his 101-mile-per-hour fastball right at my head! Would I stop teaching and ponder my response? Would I begin talking to myself, saying, "Well, let's see. Randy Johnson just launched a 101-mile-an-hour fastball toward my nose. I suppose I should start thinking about getting out of the way"? I don't think so! Much faster than you could say "Randy Johnson," my hands would fly up in front of my face to block this attack on my life! I wouldn't need to think about it. I wouldn't even be conscious of what I had done until I felt the impact of the baseball on my wrists. The reaction would be automatic.

Just as there are natural defense mechanisms at the physical level, so there are natural defense mechanisms at the emotional and psychological level. If someone says something hurtful about us, we may react defensively without even being aware that we have done so. We are quick to defend our honor and reputation even when we argue loud and long that we are not acting defensively!

At a basic level, these defense mechanisms are self-deceptions. When things go wrong, when we fail at something important, or when we are under verbal or emotional attack, we move quickly to our own defense, whether we intend to or not. In other words, we have ways of deceiving ourselves so that we can hang on to our self-esteem and avoid guilt and pain. Defense mechanisms help us avoid feeling bad about ourselves. And if knowing the truth is going to make us feel bad about ourselves, most of us would prefer not to know the truth!

Defense mechanisms are so natural that they can even be quite funny, because we recognize ourselves when we hear about them. Let me share a good example of a defense mechanism from the Bible. According to the biblical account, Saul was trying to kill David. But what does Saul do? He goes around telling everybody *that David was lying in wait to kill him!* (see 1 Samuel 22:8, 13; 24:9) This is a defense mechanism called "projection." Saul didn't want to think of himself as a brutal murderer. So he projected on to David the evil motivations that he himself was acting on. Anytime you feel bad about yourself, it's easy to start blaming everybody else.

Another defense mechanism is called "displacement." The boss hollers at you at work. But you can't talk back to the boss; you'll probably get fired if you do. So you go home and holler at your spouse instead. Your spouse doesn't want to deal with you right now, so he or she hollers at the children instead of at you. The children have been taught not to talk back to their parents, so they kick the dog in frustration. That's called "displacement." You express anger toward some person or situation, but the anger is really directed at a totally different person or situation. Displacement can come full circle only if your boss comes over to dinner, and the dog bites him!

Another defense mechanism is known as "sublimation." Sublimation occurs when a person has urges inside that are socially unacceptable. Sublimation helps a person channel those unacceptable urges into expressions that are socially acceptable. For example, a young man might have a murderous anger toward his father. But it is socially unacceptable to murder your father (not to mention being contrary to the law of God). So the young man channels this urge into a more acceptable path. He may go into hunting or he may become a football player. Violence in these fields is commended! The young man might even become a surgeon! Now don't get me wrong; I didn't say that all surgeons have a murderous anger toward their fathers! I'm simply pointing out that many of us don't fully understand all the reasons why we do what we do. Many a sweet, thoughtful young man turns into a raging animal on the football field. One might well ask where that rage comes from.

The Minirth-Meier Clinic, a well-known Christian psychiatric institute, has produced a book, *Introduction to Psychology and Counseling*. It contains a section called "The Mechanisms of Defense." This section makes a number of points about defense mechanisms with supporting evidence from the Bible. Let me share a few:

1. Defense mechanisms are automatic reactions to frustration and conflict. They move into action without our thought or intention. We have all experienced these at an emotional level, just as we have experienced physical reactions like flinching from a flying baseball. Somebody says just one little word in just the right tone of voice—and we turn around and react strongly! We didn't plan to do that. We sometimes call these incidents "red buttons." It is as if someone presses a red button, and we react in a predictable fashion. The reaction is automatic.

2. Defense mechanisms are unconscious. Most of the time we don't even know we're employing them. They are inner ways of protecting us from painful emotions and experiences. For example, we may find ourselves rejecting people who have problems similar to our own, because they remind us of ourselves in painful ways (see Romans 2:1-3). This dynamic is very common in parents, because no one is more like you than are your children. Parents are often unaware of the reasons that they react negatively toward their children.

3. *The inner purpose of defense mechanisms is to maintain a false sense of self-esteem and to avoid anxiety.* Because we don't feel good about ourselves, our self-esteem is low. And we will do whatever it takes to keep our self-esteem from getting lower. By nature, we avoid probing our innermost motives for fear that we will find something that produces guilt and makes us even feel worse about ourselves. Although defense mechanisms can protect us from the overwhelming impact of abuse or emotional pain, it is healthier to allow God, over time, to reveal to us the truth about ourselves, so that we can gain genuine freedom.

4. *Defense mechanisms are sinful, because all types of deception are sin.* The presence of defense mechanisms indicates that most human thoughts, goals, desires, and motives are selfish, destructive, and distorted. The sinful nature is written in our nerves; it is written into the very fibers of our being. In a sinful world, it is natural to be self-centered and defensive. Scripture (Jeremiah 17:9) clearly states this diagnosis: "The heart is deceitful above all things and beyond cure. Who can understand it?"

The heart is deceitful

This text is like the final blow. Not only is your heart deceitful, not only is my heart deceitful, we don't even know how deceitful our hearts are! There's only one conclusion I can draw from everything we've seen in this chapter: To be real is a supernatural event. When you find a truly authentic person, you know that they have been face-to-face with God. And I would take it a step further. No one can possibly be real unless his self-worth is built on something other than himself. If your self-esteem is based on your performance, then you're afraid to be real because you suspect that your performance is less than perfect. As you look down deep inside, you know that you'll find things that you don't really want to know about. In a purely human sense, therefore, there is no such thing as being real. Every act of sinful humanity is a deception.

"But wait a minute," you may be thinking. "Maybe we have problems with authenticity in the church, but I know lots of secular people who are genuine and authentic." And it is probably true. Secular people do seem to find it easier to talk about their faults than do most Christians. Secular people often seem less burdened with hang-ups than is the typical church person. There is quite a bit of authenticity in the outside world.

But there is so much less at stake in the secular world. For Seventh-day Adventists, every thought, every word, every action has eternal consequences. And not only that, you are often being watched by critical eyes. Under all that pressure, it can be very, very easy to play games. It can be easy to put on a mask. And we may be tempted to wear a mask as a way of life. So even though there seems to be more authenticity in the secular world, self-deception is not absent there, either. It is just masked by the lower stakes that are involved.

Do we have to?

If authenticity is impossible in our human strength, we may be tempted to stop trying to be authentic. Wouldn't it make more sense just to find a mask that won't slip off when we're in trouble? Wouldn't it be an "ideal world" if everyone could totally, successfully hide themselves? Well, if you are at all tempted by this idea, I have bad news for you. Authenticity is not an option. We cannot walk away from this challenge and still stay alive spiritually. Notice the words of Jesus in John 3:21.

> "But whoever practices the truth
> comes into the light,
> in order that his works might be manifested
> that they were worked through God."

John 3:20 tells us that people outside of Christ seek the darkness. They seek to hide. But according to verse 21, those in Christ are different. They come out into the light. They are open and honest about their failings. And out of that honesty comes a wonderful realization: When troubled, messed up people do anything right, it is because God is working in their lives!

Christian authenticity brings glory to God—not to the human agent. Because when human agents are authentic, you know that they make mistakes. And you know that they know that they make mistakes. So, if a preacher or an administrator is no better than you or me, whatever good they do must be a miracle from God! And the glory for that action goes to God—not the human agent.

Authenticity is not merely an option for Christians. The minute we put on a mask, we are being someone we are not. We are trying to make ourselves look better than we really are. To the extent that we succeed, we steal the glory that belongs to God. That is the ultimate self-deception, the root of the sin in Lucifer's heart way back in the beginning. Not only that, lack of authenticity drives people away from Christ instead of drawing them to Him.

I once asked a youth group, "What is it about the church that presents the greatest barrier to your staying a Christian when you reach adulthood?" They each answered privately. And most of them said essentially the same thing: "People who act as if they had no faults."

What an irony! We want to set a good example for young people. We want to show them the joys of church life. So we struggle to hide our defects and our doubts. We put forth the image of a "good Adventist" whether or not we feel it in our hearts. We put on a mask of Christian faithfulness and success. And the young people see right through that mask. Not only does it fail to work, it drives them out of the church faster than anything else we could do.

What shall we do, then, with our doubts and defects? Shall we revel in them and spread them around as a mark of our authenticity?

That isn't the answer either. In my experience, sharing our present doubts and defects tends to be discouraging to others. It can even

doubts & failures

incline them toward dangerous behaviors and ideas. The first step in ministering to others is to become aware of our defects and to take them to God for forgiveness and healing. To share current failure is to discourage others. On the other hand, to share struggles in areas in which we are making progress, can give others the courage to deal with their own struggles.

Lack of authenticity also destroys our spiritual growth. Our masks keep us from seeing the very shortcomings that we need to bring to Christ for healing. While authenticity doesn't earn us salvation, lack of authenticity can cause us to lose our salvation. After all, we are saved only to the extent that we confess our sins, to the extent that we admit we need what God has to offer. Confession is simply telling the truth about ourselves. Not to confess is to tell a dangerous lie before God who already knows the full truth about us.

Lack of Authenticity in relationships

Another reason that a lack of authenticity is not an option for Christians is that it destroys our relationships. In a marriage, people often go out of their way to keep on masks. When problems arise, we try to smooth them over and keep the peace. An inauthentic marriage can last twenty years or more. All the neighbors think it's the perfect family. One day, the husband comes home and finds his wife angrily packing suitcases.

"I've had enough!" she says.

The husband replies, "What's the matter?"

Lack of Authenticity in finances

"I don't need to tell you; you know what's wrong!"

"But, I don't know! What's going on here?"

That's what a lack of authenticity does. We hide, and we hide, and the problems get bigger and bigger. One day, it all blows up in our faces, and then it's too late to resolve.

Lack of authenticity is also destructive in the area of personal finances. A good example is the problem of credit cards. You can buy anything—up to half your annual income, it seems—with a credit card, and not pay a cent for it up front. Oh, yes, there's a bill that comes next month. But the credit card company wants only a few dollars. In the meantime, it's as if you get all these things free! But nothing is really free. One day, reality strikes. In financial terms, authenticity means having a budget. It means knowing where every dollar is going. If you don't want to be financially authentic—and most people don't—the obligations pile up and pile up until you're at disaster's door.

The same thing is true with our health. We don't want to be authentic about our health. We like to imagine that we can eat anything we want, sit around all day, ignore all the rules of health, and still live to be a hundred without a single illness. But that's not real life. Lack of authenticity can kill you, and you'll probably be the last one to know about it before you go. Authenticity is not just an option for Christians; in most areas of existence, authenticity is a matter of life and death for us.

But there is one major problem with authenticity. We don't know how to achieve it. Our hearts are deceitful, and we don't even know how deceitful they are! Being real is the most difficult thing we've ever tried to do.

It seems to me that there are two major barriers to being real. First, we don't know our condition, the depth of our self-deception. Until we see ourselves clearly, we don't even know when we are faking it.

Second, we don't have a sense of our true value before God. A poor sense of self-worth, a deep inner perception that we are hopeless and worthless, prevents us from being real. So if we are to understand our self-deception, if we are to have a clear picture of our own depravity, we must first of all have a genuine sense of our value.

Our value before God

Because sin is deeply ingrained in every fiber of our being, the more we know about ourselves, the more we dislike ourselves—and the worse we feel. When self-worth is low, the most natural thing in the world is for us to put out an image rather than submit to reality. How, then, can we elevate our sense of self-worth? As we saw in the very first chapter of this book, self-worth must be grounded in a relationship with Jesus Christ. Any other path to self-worth will ultimately disappoint.

This is why the gospel is so central to everything that we do in life. Without the gospel it is impossible to believe that God can value us. Without knowledge of the gospel, we have no choice but to project our own sense of damage and worthlessness onto God and believe that He despises us as much as we despise ourselves. The only path to self-worth, then, comes in the gospel of acceptance in Christ at the Cross. It is at the Cross that we find out how valuable we are to God.

Let's look a little deeper into this issue. A close friend of mine, Ed Dickerson, offers a helpful analysis of the human need for self-worth. He believes that self-worth is based on three life convictions—(1) I am precious, (2) I am unique, and (3) I am capable. To be fully conscious of all three is to have a secure sense of worth. But very few of us have any sense of our preciousness, our uniqueness, or our capability because all through life we have heard messages that contradict those convictions.

If a child could grow up knowing that he is precious, it would provide a strong foundation for self-worth. But instead of being told that they are precious, most children hear very different messages. "You are worthless." "You're a slut." "You're so selfish." The message is drummed into them that they have no special value, that they are only tolerated by others, that they are not precious to others.

Instead of hearing the message that they are unique, most children hear, "You're just like all the rest." On the rare occasions when their uniqueness is noticed, it is the object of scorn: "I'm sure glad there is no one else just like you; I don't think the universe could handle it!"

Instead of being affirmed for the many talents and gifts that God has given them, most kids hear messages such as, "Your best isn't good enough" (don't I know that!). Or "Can't you ever do anything right?" Or "You're so lazy that by the time you finish this job the dog will be dead!" From day one, life presents us with an unrelenting assault on our self-worth. And this is not to blame everything on parents. (I don't need that; I already am one!) But parents and others who deal with children are often just projecting their own sense of worthlessness as they interact with them. So, unless we can deal with our lack of self-worth, we compound the problem in the next generation.

But thank God there is a way out. At the Cross God sent a very different message to the human race. The gospel says, "You are absolutely precious. You are worth the whole universe to God." The same Jesus who died on the cross is the Creator of the entire universe. So when Jesus died for me, His sacrifice carried the value of everything in the entire universe! What an incredible value God has placed on you and me! We are so precious to Him that He was willing to sacrifice His Son for you and me. So the gospel of Jesus Christ tells us that we are infinitely precious.

The gospel also tells us that we are unique. We are told that Jesus would have gone to the cross even if only one person needed saving! He'd have died just for you! That tells me that our uniqueness is very important to God. The same God who made no two snowflakes exactly alike, made no two human beings exactly alike. That means that every human being is a witness to a unique facet of God's character and of His plan for the human race. Every time a person is lost for eternity, there is an eternal loss that cannot be fully replaced! We are truly unique—preciously so!

The gospel also tells us that we are capable. Whenever a person comes into a saving relationship with Jesus, he receives spiritual gifts through the working of the Holy Spirit. No two people have exactly the same mix of gifts, but everyone has some gift. And those gifts are powerful enablings from God that empower us to make a real difference in the world.

So at the Cross we find a true sense of our value. In the gospel we come to know that we are precious, unique, and capable. In our relationship with Jesus we find a self-worth that cannot be taken away from us. And that is the key to Christian authenticity. In the acceptance that we find in Jesus, we can begin to lift the lid on the darkness within. We can begin a journey toward authenticity, honesty, and self-discovery.

Basic steps to authenticity

What are the basic steps in the journey toward being real? In my experience, the path to authenticity can be summarized in five steps. These five steps are worth memorizing, so that you can go over them again and again and make them a part of your daily walk with God.

1. Know your true condition. You cannot become authentic unless you are willing to face the truth about yourself. We will have more to say about this as an ongoing process in the next major section of this chapter.

2. Accept the truth about yourself. Accept the reality that you've been "faking it." When you come to realize the full depth of your depravity and your sin, accept that it is a true statement of your condition.

3. Take the truth about yourself to Christ for forgiveness and release. You take it to Him by confessing it. You tell Him the truth about yourself, no matter how painful that might be. What's to stop you? He already knows everything about you. There is nothing you could tell Him that He does not know. But when you confess to Him the reality of your sin, two wonderful things happen. First, there's forgiveness. There is the recognition that He accepts you as you are, even in your darkness. Second, there is release from the power of that sin. There's something about confessing your past that takes away its power. Your past can no longer define you because Jesus will take its power away, if you will only be open and honest about it.

4. Accept, by God's grace, that you are significant and valuable in Christ. When it comes to authenticity, this is perhaps the most important of the five basic steps. Only a person who knows that he or she is valuable would ever dare to examine the darkness within. The only way we can gain that knowledge is through the gospel. Our value is defined at the Cross. Out of that sense of value comes the drive to be real. On the other hand, the moment that we feel unaccepted by God, the masks go on immediately. No human being is capable of being truly authentic in his or her own strength. Only in the strength that we receive from Christ can we accomplish this work.

5. Seek to grow continually in authenticity. Authenticity is a process, not a state. No human being can become totally authentic in a moment. It would kill us if we could. Our nerves couldn't handle it. So God feeds us the bad news a little bit at a time. And in the courage of Christ, we can face a little bit each time. As we grow in a relationship with Him, we become more and more real. Authenticity is a relationship. It is living out in practice what God has said about us on the cross. Because I matter to God, I matter also to me. If God values me, then I had better value myself.

No one can value others unless he senses some value in himself. Christians, who are bitter, cynical, and faultfinding, have little or no sense of their own value. Although they may have been in the church for fifty years or more, they have no clear grasp of the gospel. They do not know the Jesus that they are seeking to protect by their criticism.

The struggle to "know thyself"

Although the most important of the five steps listed above is number four—the affirmation about the gospel—the most difficult step is the first. It is knowing the truth about ourselves. I remind you of the long pilgrimage I shared with you at the beginning of this chapter. Time and time again, I was sure that I had attained authenticity—only to discover a hidden phoniness right in the midst of my best efforts to be real.

Anyone who has struggled for authenticity knows how difficult it is to grasp. You can have it, and twenty-four hours later find yourself faking it again. How do we make our way to a clear picture of our own reality? How do we find true authenticity when the evident reality about ourselves is self-deception (see Jeremiah 17:9)? Let me share a series of practical steps to self-knowledge—things I have learned over the last thirty years in the greatest battle of my life. My struggle will have been well worth it, if it can be the means of helping others.

1. Spend time with the Word of God. One step in the path toward authenticity is to spend as much time as you can reading the Word of God. This may seem an obvious place to start. However, many people who read their Bibles daily, are still not confronted by their own self-deception. We need, therefore, to unpack this concept further.

First of all, the Bible aids our search for authenticity by affirming our value before God. As you read its pages, look for the many ways that the gospel comes through. Mark the passages that talk about how much God values you. Many of us have been raised in a legalistic setting in which the gospel is affirmed in speech but not believed in experience. We qualify every statement of the gospel to the point that it doesn't seem truly biblical—"we are saved by faith apart from any works, but . . ." It is imperative, therefore, that we saturate ourselves in the biblical texts that affirm the gospel until every legalistic doubt in our minds is driven away. This process can take quite a bit of time. Only when we know and understand the gospel will we have the courage to enter into the process of growing self-awareness.

Further help to our search for self-awareness can be found in the Bible's biographies, the stories about its major characters. It's a good thing that I didn't write the Bible, because I would probably have treated the main characters of the Bible as heroes. Abraham, Moses, David, and others could easily have been portrayed as flawless saints. I would have told about their wonderful deeds so that other people would be encouraged. But instead of being encouraged, those striving for authenticity would have come away from the Bible discouraged. They would have felt that they could never attain the kind of relationship with God that these biblical heroes had experienced. And they would be tempted to give up the struggle.

But I didn't write the Bible; God directed its production. Character after character is portrayed authentically, as a real person with significant flaws. In fact, most Bible characters seem even more messed up than you or I. Yet God used them. He didn't wait for them to become perfect lest His reputation be soiled by association with them. He used them in spite of their flaws. This characteristic of the Bible's biographies is powerfully described in one of the most remarkable passages in Ellen White's writings (see *Testimonies for the Church*, vol. 4, pp. 9-11).

the Story of Esther

The story of Esther is an example. Because the hard edges of the story are not that plain in translation, we have had a tendency to elevate Esther to a certain level of sainthood. She is the brave girl, who by the grace of God, won a beauty contest and became a faithful witness to truth in the pagan king's court. I don't doubt that she was brave. But the Hebrew text of the book makes it clear that it was no beauty contest and that Esther was no example of how to practice faith in a hostile environment.

Whether or not Esther chose to be a candidate in the "contest," it was not about beauty. The contest involved a "one-night stand" with the king. And she participated, evidently with enthusiasm. Esther somehow proved that she was better in bed than all the other girls. In Hebrew, Esther 2:13, 14 say that in the evening the girls would go to the king from the House of the Virgins, and in the morning they would go to the House of the Concubines. Most translations gloss over this in embarrassment. If you find yourself offended by this story, take it up with the Author. He may prove to be more open-minded than we are.

Not only did Esther become queen by this unusual means, it is also clear that she did not practice her faith when she lived in the palace (see Esther 2:10; 5:12, 13; 7:3, 4). There is no mention of God or prayer anywhere in the book. Evidently, Esther stopped keeping the Sabbath and didn't eat the special Jewish diet. She was a "cultural Jew." How do we know? Her own husband didn't have a clue that she was Jewish. Authentic Jews are very hard to hide, especially if they are living in your own bedroom and kitchen.

You see, Esther and Mordecai weren't even supposed to be in Persia. God had called His people out of Babylon (and Persia) fifty years before. Many had gone back to Palestine under God's direction. Most did not. Life had become comfortable, and God's call seemed more than they could bear. Esther and Mordecai were representatives of a whole people out of line with God's commands. And once the road to compromise is entered, it can be hard to get off, and one can end up in surprising places.

But in spite of all the shady things that went on, what do we know about Esther? When the people of God faced a great crisis, she was in the right place at the right time to accomplish God's purpose. Although His people were in apostasy, God did not abandon them. Although Esther's life was full of small and large compromises, God was still willing to use her. She was truly a heroine of courage in spite of her faults. What a God we serve! No matter where you've been, no matter what you've done, God can still work miracles in your life if you will let Him. No matter how dark the discoveries you make in your quest for authenticity, God is willing and able to redeem your life and use you for His glory.

The Bible is an authentic book. Even in translation, 2 Samuel will knock your socks off. As far as Hollywood goes, 2 Samuel is definitely R-rated for sex and violence. However, in the Bible, unlike Hollywood, the sex and the violence are there to show us the folly of a life apart from God and the pain that comes when we violate the laws of our being. And they are there to encourage us that, like David, we can break away from the darkness to a better way of life.

An honest reading of the Bible, therefore, should lead us to authenticity and give us the courage to confess our sins. If God could accept Esther and David, there's hope that He'll accept me, too. But by itself, reading the Bible is not enough. Have you ever read your Bible for fifteen minutes or so and then realized that you couldn't remember a thing you had read? Defense mechanisms don't shut down just because we are reading the Bible. In fact, we all have a tendency to see what we want to see when we are reading the Bible. I have learned, gradually, that I cannot find full authenticity in Bible study alone. I needed to combine it with something else.

2. Practice authentic prayer. A crucial companion to authentic Bible study is authentic prayer. When we offer authentic prayer in the context of Bible study, there is some hope that we will learn something from the Bible. Authentic Christians find something fresh in the Word every day because they are open to God's "jarring" in the spirit.

Authentic prayer is not just any kind of prayer. What I mean by authentic prayer is prayer that is directed toward God in full commitment. It is a whole-hearted, whole-souled immersion in the prayer

Truth

experience. Authentic prayer says, "I want to know the truth, no matter what the cost." When we seek truth in the Bible, we need to allow God to open us up to His Spirit, to make us willing to know the truth, accept the truth, and follow the truth wherever it leads. When you tell God, "I want the truth, no matter what the cost," you will receive it—but you will also pay the cost. Truth can cost you your family, your job, your reputation. Truth can even cost you your life. Do you want to know the truth that much? If you do, God will give it to you.

In my previous book, *Present Truth in the Real World*, I tell of a time when I was wrestling to know God's will in my life. I was lying face down on a hardwood floor in Brooklyn. I didn't know what to do. Finally, in desperation I cried out to God, "I want the truth, the whole truth, and nothing but the truth, and I don't care what it costs me!" And God gave me what I needed. My life has never been the same.

3. Apply the various types of journaling. A close companion to authentic prayer is journaling, a subject we covered in some detail a few chapters back. In journaling, I seek to let God open me up to my true self. God uses writing to draw up the depths of my being in ways that nothing else can. I can use jounrnaling to pray, to record God's answers to prayer, and to take note of the various ways in which God's power has been at work in my life. But the journal that is most pertinent to the issue of authenticity is the Book of Experience. Here I invite God to probe whatever area of my life He wishes to examine, and to expose me to it in writing! This has been an invaluable experience in developing authenticity.

I've discovered, however, that self-deception is an incredibly sneaky thing. You can deceive yourself even in your own diary! I remember a day when I was writing in my journal and really going deep. The thought suddenly came to me, "What if you were to die tonight and the whole world would see what you wrote in this journal?" So I started editing it a little to make it look a little better! Not very smart, but very human! No one wants others to think badly of them, even after death. So journaling, as helpful as it is, is not the final answer by itself.

4. Take authentic prayer another level deeper. We've talked about wanting the truth no matter what the cost. And that is tremendously important. But when it comes to knowing yourself, it isn't good enough. I have learned to go to an even deeper level of prayer. One could call this deeper level of authentic prayer "Authentic Prayer II: The Sequel"! This prayer goes something like this: "Lord, I want the truth *about myself,* no matter what the cost."

Do you see the difference? Truth can be very abstract. Truth can be doctrinal. Truth can be about gaining a right understanding of all the beasts of Revelation and having them organized in a row. Knowing truth can be very satisfying. But it can become a substitute for a more practical kind of truth. Knowing the truth about myself is very different from truth in the abstract. It comes very, very close to home. It is the kind of knowledge about ourselves that other people often have. So you could pray this way: "Lord, help me to see myself as other people see me. Help me to get the kind of understanding about myself that other people have."

God is very good at that. Hebrews 4 tells us that He's a "heart" surgeon who gets down deep inside. He can even divide the bone from the marrow. He can dig even deeper to see the thoughts and intents of the heart. The book *Steps to Christ* contains a most precious statement: "The closer you come to Jesus, the more faulty you will appear in your own eyes" (page 64). In practice, many people have turned that statement around. They act as if it says, "The closer you come to Jesus, the more faulty will everyone else appear in your own eyes." But, that's not reality.

Those who are close to Jesus are very much aware of their own faults, so much so that they don't have time for the faults of anyone else. One of the clearest signs of a dying Christian experience is a critical and fault-finding spirit. But although authentic prayer is a very valuable tool, I've learned that even the deepest levels of authentic prayer sometimes don't go deep enough. I've learned that we can deceive ourselves even in prayer. For example, have you ever lied to God in prayer? Have you ever gone to church so mad at God that you wanted to punch Him in the nose? But when it came your turn to pray, you said something like, "Oh, Lord, I love You so much. You are so important to me." It's truly amazing! We know that God knows all about us, yet we tell Him what we think He wants to hear! So our search for authenticity needs to go even deeper than the prayer life—even deeper than journaling and Bible study.

5. Accountability. The deepest level of all may be the most critical to success in knowing oneself—accountability. Self-deception is rooted deeply enough in all of us that it is intertwined even into our prayer lives and our Bible study. Sometimes, the only way that God can break through to us is through another human being.

> There are souls perplexed with doubt, burdened with infirmities, weak in faith, and unable to grasp the Unseen; but a friend whom they can see, coming to them in Christ's stead, can be a connecting link to fasten their trembling faith upon Christ (Ellen G. White, *The Desire of Ages*, p. 297).

Accountability means allowing others to help you keep watch over yourself. There are a number of ways that you can take advantage of this. One way is through a sharing group like Alcoholics Anonymous or a "cell church" in which the only penalty is for not being authentic. Everybody is required to tell the truth and is accepted in their telling of it. And a fascinating thing happens in a group like that. As you hear someone else telling the truth about himself, you connect with what he is saying and realize that you have some of those same faults yourself. You recognize yourself in the confession of another. In an atmosphere in which people are confessing their sins, you have the courage to confess your own.

This is a real struggle for Seventh-day Adventists. Prayer groups in the Adventist Church often fail because of a lack of authenticity. We are quick to make prayer requests for other people, particularly people who are at some distance from our active concerns: "My neighbor's wife has a nephew whose third cousin's boss has been diagnosed with cancer. Please pray for him." Or our requests for ourselves are inconsequential (and therefore safe): "Pray that God will give me ten dollars to buy a new hair-dryer."

The deep problems that we worry about in the dark tend to be left unspoken. By making relatively inconsequential requests we can maintain the illusion of authenticity while protecting ourselves from painful scrutiny by others. My wife once belonged to a women's small group in our church. To encourage authenticity, a rule was established: No one could ask for prayer for anyone else or speak about anyone else's problems. Any request must be either for themselves or related to their own needs (a spouse's illness can have a frightful impact on oneself). It was a powerful group.

Related to this concept of small groups is an insight from Seventh-day Adventist history. A friend suggested it to me. Many of the testimonies in Ellen White's *Testimonies for the Church* read as if they came from the journals of the people to whom they were written. In these testimonies God was offering a unique path to authenticity, telling people truths about themselves that they had failed to understand on their own. Perhaps the purpose of these testimonies is not so much to be unbending rules for all who read them as to do the work of a small group in the readers' own quest for accountability. In reading the *Testimonies* we can often identify with things that Ellen White was saying to someone else. The *Testimonies,* rightly handled, can open up windows into our own depravity to which we can apply the gospel for forgiveness and healing.

I have an even scarier suggestion for the few and the brave. Find a carefully-selected (hard-nosed) friend who loves you and cares deeply about you. Someone who would never want to see you hurt. Go to this friend and tell him or her, "If you knew that I wouldn't get mad and take it out on you later, what would you tell me about myself? What problems do you see in my relationship with God? How do I come across to other people?"

That is scary, isn't it? Well, I couldn't live without it. I have three such friends, in addition to my wife. One is White, one is Black, and the third is Hispanic. I know that these three men love me, and I trust their love. I have given them the right to confront me about my faults at any time. Whenever we get together, we have accountability sessions in which we go away alone together and open up to each other the deepest recesses of our hearts. The Bible says, "Nothing is so precious as the wounds of a friend" (Proverbs 27:6). And no friend is so true as one who loves you enough to tell you the truth about yourself.

You see, I am somewhat of a public person. Many people are a bit afraid of me because I have a very strong personality. The average person tends to tell me what they think I want to hear. But I don't want to end up like Saddam Hussein. No one ever tells him the truth, because the advisors who tell him the truth are dead! So when Saddam Hussein is making a big mistake, he is probably the last person to know it. Too many people are depending on me and my walk with God. So I've worked very hard to cultivate friends that I can trust and to encourage them to be honest with me. This is one of the best ways to bypass your own defense mechanisms.

But what if you don't have any close friends? What if there is no one on this earth that you would trust with the deepest anguish of your heart? There is still a way. Find a good, Christian counselor to help you. Counselors are trained to help people open up and discover the deeper truths about themselves. Counselors are trained to be good listeners. Counselors can often detect when you are playing games of self-deception. Counselors are trained to offer the kind of accountability we need in the context of confidentiality. While I have found counseling helpful at various stages of my life, it is particularly critical for those who have nowhere else to turn. Life is too short to waste in unauthenticity.

CONCLUSION

For the sake of reaching those who don't know God, Christians, particularly Seventh-day Adventist Christians, are tempted to craft an image of high-quality Christian faith. We want secular people to see our church as an ideal community in which their lives can be set free from the strife and confusion of the real world. We want the church to be truly attractive to them. So we try to hide our doubts and our conflicts for the sake of secular seekers. We fear that authenticity, since it reveals our "bad stuff," is opposed to being a good witness.

However, when it comes to influencing secular people, truth is good. Being authentic is the best way to reach secular people with the gospel because it allows them to identify with us. Secular people have come to believe that church is a cop out, a way of avoiding painful realities. But when they see broken people following Jesus, it jars their misconceptions about Christian faith. When they see real people finding faith, they are tempted to try it for themselves. When secular people discover that even Jesus, who was without sin, was at times needy, angry, sad, and frustrated, they become open to a relationship with Him. When Christians are authentic, therefore, it gives seekers reason to hope that they too might be welcome to approach the throne of God.

So, for Christians who want to know God for themselves and who wish to reach out to their neighbors in the real world, the road to authenticity is the only way to go. It is certainly a tough road, leading straight up the side of a mountain. It begins at the foot of the Cross with the realization that we are worth the whole universe to Him. If we are worth that much to Him, then it doesn't matter what anyone else thinks about us. With the courage we receive in Christ, we can begin groping toward honesty and reality.

While you may feel discouraged at the enormity of the task, let me remind you that there is One who knows everything there is to know about you—and He knew it all before He decided to go to the Cross. As He pondered the depths of your soul, He could have easily said, "Ohhhh, I'm not going to die for that!" Instead, He spread His arms out to you and to the whole world. He says, "I embrace you as you are. I embrace you with all your shortcomings. I embrace you with all your self-deceptions. I embrace you with all your defense mechanisms. And if you will let Me, I want to elevate you to sit with Me on My throne to be among the most honored people in the entire universe (see Revelation 3:21). In Me, you have everything you need."

At the foot of the Cross, you can begin to let the mask slip down. You can begin to let your real self show, because you can also talk about the value you have in Jesus. There is no way out of the human dilemma without Jesus. As you read these concluding words, I want to invite you to give yourself unreservedly to Jesus in the quiet of your own thoughts. What are you really giving up anyway? What is there to lose? What you're giving Him is the confusion and the self-deception that you'd love to get rid of anyway. Receive Him and welcome a new day of self-awareness mixed with peace.

Many of us dream that the Church will take up its God-ordained role for the end time and prepare the world for the return of Jesus. But the only kind of church that will make a major difference in today's world is one in which the people and the faith are real. This is no easy task, but today is as good a day as any to start. Today can be the beginning of a more authentic Christian faith in your life. I invite you to join me on the path. The road is steep, but you're going to love the view!

If you enjoyed this book, you'll enjoy these as well:

Present Truth in the Real World
Jon Paulien. This exciting book discusses the Adventist struggle
to keep and share faith in a secular society. If taken to heart, it
could prove to be the catalyst that launches the greatest success
Adventists have ever experienced in reaching the unreached.
0-8163-1127-7. Paperback. US$10.99, Cdn$16.49.

The Millennium Bug
Jon Paulien. The author boldly rebuts those who have reached
conclusions about the beginning of the new millennium that are
unsupported by the Bible and the Spirit of Prophecy, and shows
how we can maintain the proper balance between expectancy
and "occupying" until the Lord comes.
0-8163-1755-0. Paperback. US$9.99, Cdn$14.99.

Your Religion is Too Small
Steven Mosley. Through many real-life stories of great men and
women of faith, Steven Mosley calls us to break out of a small
view of faith and embrace a life of creative, virtuous living that
expands our witness, and makes a real difference in the world.
0-8163-1782-8. Paperback. US$11.99, Cdn$17.99.

Order from your ABC by calling **1-800-765-6955**, or get online
and shop our virtual store at **<www.adventistbookcenter.com>**.

Read a chapter from your favorite book

Order online

Sign up for email notices on new products